British Virgin Islands

Islands

ALIVE!

Harriet & Douglas Greenberg

HUNTER

Hunter Publishing, Inc.
130 Campus Drive
Edison, NJ 08818-7816
☎ 732-225-1900 / 800-255-0343 / Fax 732-417-1744
www.hunterpublishing.com
comments@hunterpublishing.com

IN CANADA
Ulysses Travel Publications
4176 Saint-Denis, Montréal, Québec, Canada H2W 2M5
☎ 514-843-9882 ext. 2232 / Fax 514-843-9448

IN THE UK
Windsor Books International
The Boundary, Wheatley Road, Garsington,
Oxford OX44 9EJ England
☎ 01865-361122 / Fax 01865-361133

Printed in the United States of America
ISBN 1-58843-507-5
© 2005 Hunter Publishing, Inc.

Front Cover: Virgin Gorda (Digital Vision Ltd.)
Back Cover: Tortola (www.imivi.com)
Maps by Kim André, © 2005 Hunter Publishing, Inc.
Index by Nancy Wolff

Contents

Maps

The Caribbean

N

Atlantic Ocean

VIRGIN ISLANDS

PUERTO
RICO

Anguilla

Barbuda
Antigua
Guadeloupe
Dominica
Martinique

Barbados

St. Kitts & Nevis

St. Lucia
St. Vincent
Grenada

Trinidad & Tobago

Tortuga
Margarita

DOMINICAN
REPUBLIC

HAITI

Curaçao

Aruba

Bahama Islands

CUBA

Caribbean Sea

VENEZUELA

GUYANA

JAMAICA

COLOMBIA

Florida

PANAMA

COSTA
RICA

NICARAGUA

HONDURAS

NOT TO SCALE

Introduction

I must go down to the sea again
To the beautiful sea and the sky
And all I ask is a sailing ship
And a star to sail her by

The opening lines to this John Mansfield poem often run through my mind when I think of the British Virgin Islands. For life is sea-centered on the 50 or so volcanic isles, rocks and cays here. The tall ships that sail here today, dropping anchor for a short swim, were predated by the ships of pirates who lurked here awaiting treasure-laden galleons on their way to Europe.

The principal islands are clustered around the Sir Francis Drake Channel in two parallel strands. On the north are the large islands, Tortola and Beef, while the south strand includes many small islands such as Norman, Peter, Salt and Cooper, plus Virgin Gorda. The positioning of the islands creates a protected channel 20 miles long and five miles wide, with some of the finest sailing waters in the world. Two of the larger islands not on the channel are Jost Van Dyke, northwest of Tortola, and Anegada, 20 miles north of Virgin Gorda.

Only a handful of the islands have accommodations for tourists and these, in keeping with the BVI's character, are small, picturesque and private. The largest number, on Tortola, are set on beachfronts, in ancient fortresses, ruins of sugar mills and on mountainsides.

On Virgin Gorda, Little Dix Bay is as charming a stop as I've ever seen without being glitzy, while nearby Peter Island Resort, on its own island, is special as well. Several of the largely uninhabited is-

The Virgin Islands

lands have excellent restaurants, lively nightspots and some accommodations as well. These have sprung up to service visitors aboard yachts and are located at stunning anchorage sites.

Determined to protect their magnificent natural resources, the British Virgin Islands National Parks Trust has designated 11 areas as national parks, with 10 others under consideration. Among these are marine parks, including The Baths on Virgin Gorda. The Baths, the single most visited stop in the BVI, is a unique rock formation that includes underwater grottos just right for snorkeling.

While nothing equals the fervor of sailing here, scuba diving is making a race of it. These are over 60 charted dive sites, with ghostly sunken ships, pinnacles and caves to be explored.

There are a surprising number of good restaurants and no visit to the BVI would be complete without a tall, cool drink made with the island's own Pusser's rum. For over 300 years (1655 to 1970) sailors of Britain's Royal Navy were issued a daily ration of rum by the purser, pronounced "pusser" by the Jack Tars. Pusser's a blend of five West Indian rums, makes a delicious Fuzzy Naval.

Small and sparsely populated, the islands remain relatively untouched by tourism – no high-rise hotels, no time-share condos, no casinos. In fact not much nightlife at all. The British Virgin Islands are for laid-back people.

There are 50 islands in the group – 49 volcanic and one limestone and coral atoll. From the air a few seem large and studded with buildings, but most are tiny and uninhabited. They lie like pieces of a puzzle along the Sir Francis Drake Channel which courses through them like a liquid thoroughfare. There are approximately 21,000 British Virgin Islanders and

almost 16,000 of them live on the largest island, Tortola. Virgin Gorda houses virtually all the rest, with only a few hundred hardy souls on Jost Van Dyke, Peter Island and Anegada. Tourist accommodations and facilities are largely confined to these islands as well, although there are private island resorts and eating options at several anchorage sites.

There are no dangerous snakes in the BVI.

Chartered yachts and day-sail ships visit the uninhabited islands' pristine beaches, thriving coral reefs and interesting rock formations. You see lizards, tropical birds, mongooses and lush tropical foliage, but few humans.

Wherever you bed down, you are not limited to just one island. Frequent ferry service links the major islands with one another and with the US Virgin Islands nearby. Each of the islands has its own attractions and personality.

A Thumbnail Sketch

Tortola

The largest island, Tortola, is the hub of the chain. Road Town, a picturesque town on the island's southern shore, is both the capital of Tortola and of the BVI. All the government buildings and businesses are here. Yet Tortola is peaceful, quiet and unhurried. The island is split by a mountain range. Its northern shore has small towns and a string of stunning beaches, while the southern shore has scores of marinas and yacht charter companies.

The BVI is the yacht charter capital of the Caribbean.

Tortola has several luxurious resorts and a much larger number of small hotels and inns. There are many restaurants, including several that would be at home in New York and Los Angeles. The island's southern coast faces the channel and from it and Road Town, you can see Peter, Norman and the Dead Chest Islands, made famous by Robert Louis Stevenson.

Virgin Gorda

A ferry sprints across the channel carrying visitors to Virgin Gorda, the BVI's second-most important island. Physically stunning, the island is in the midst of a building boom. New condominium developments are being constructed at virtually every bay on the southern part of the island. This will change the character of Virgin Gorda, but will provide a much-needed boost to the economy. Flat, with giant boulders, the southern part of the island is home to

Spanish Town, the capital, and most of the island's residents. It is connected to the island's central portion by a mile-wide strip of land. This central portion is dominated by a mountain and park. The northern part of Virgin Gorda encircles North Sound, a beautiful body of water that has small islands within it and luxurious resorts that are accessible only by water.

Peter Island

This 1,800-acre island houses one resort, The Peter Island Resort and Yacht Club. It has a handful of white-sand beaches, two excellent restaurants (open to the public) and scores of activities, including tennis, bicycling and hiking. There's a fitness center and a watersports center with snorkel gear and windsurfers. The resort's private ferry service connects Peter Island to Tortola several times daily.

Jost Van Dyke

Named for a Dutch pirate, Jost Van Dyke is totally different from the other islands. It is simply a place to have fun, and a lot of beer fuels the fun. It has three settled areas that are the most popular anchorages in the BVI. There are a handful of guest cottages in each area, but the lure is the beachfront eateries/bars, which stay open well into the night. The island's most famous resident is Foxy, who owns the rowdiest club and organizes concerts and boat races that draw people from all the islands. There is daily ferry service from Tortola, but it doesn't run late into the night.

Anegada

The only non-volcanic island, Anegada is a coral and limestone slip of land surrounded by a vast coral reef. Its highest point is only 28 feet above sea level. It has a small settlement at Loblolly Bay where there are a handful of small hotels and cottages and an equal number of eateries. The island is known for its lobsters. Over 300 ships have sunk on the reef that encircles the island, but you no longer have to sail here. There is an 11-minute flight from Tortola several days a week. Anegada, 16 miles north of Virgin Gorda, is not on Sir Francis Drake Channel.

Beef Island

Famous as a buccaneer's hunting grounds, Beef Island is just 300 feet off Tortola's East End and connected to it by the Queen Elizabeth II toll bridge (50¢). Home to the BVI's international airport, Beef Island has a shell-filled beach on its northern shore. There is a marked snorkel trail as well. Trellis Bay, just beyond the airport has a guest house with a popular restaurant, Da Loose Mongoose, and a cyber café. Ferries from Trellis Bay go to the Last Resort, a British-style pub-restaurant and to Marina Cay, where Pusser's has a small hotel.

Cooper Island

The Cooper Island Beach Club is a small hotel on Machioneel Bay, the only inhabited part of the island. The beach here is lovely, with waters so clear you can see the sandy bottom covered in sea grass. Guests from hotels without beach access often are ferried to Cooper Island. It's just a few minutes from Tortola's Road Town.

Norman Island

This is a very popular anchorage spot for day-sail ships because snorkeling is excellent. It is part of the BVI National Parks system.

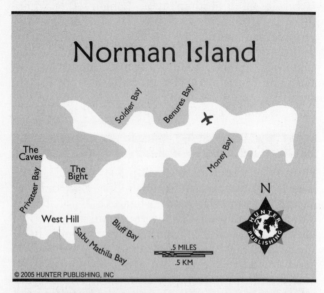

Private Islands

Guana Island, **Necker Island** and **Little Thatch** are privately owned. The resort on Guana Island is ultra-luxurious and quite small. Necker Island must be reserved by at least 25 people so it is often the site of a private event or convention. Little Thatch has a few cottages on it.

Other island names you will become familiar with include **Salt Island**, **Fallen Jerusalem**, **Great Dog** and **Little Camanoe**. Many are simply piles of rock.

Getting There

By Air

There are no non-stop flights from the US or Canada to the BVI. Most visitors fly to San Juan, Puerto Rico and connect to small local carriers for the 40-minute flight to Beef Island (Tortola) or Virgin Gorda. American Eagle, Liat, Air Sunshine and Cape Air all have daily flights from San Juan to Tortola and Air Sunshine has a daily flight to Virgin Gorda. You can also fly non-stop to St. Thomas, USVI from many cities in the US. Liat, Cape Air and Air Sunshine have daily flights from St. Thomas to Beef Island (Tortola). Book your seat on these flights when you make your original reservations. These are smaller planes. US carriers with frequent service to Puerto Rico include American Airlines, Delta Continental, US Airways and Jet Blue. All except Jet Blue also fly to St. Thomas.

Note: Do not check your bags through to Tortola. Pick them up at your initial stop and recheck them. Delayed baggage is endemic here.

By Air & Sea

If small planes are not your cup of tea, consider flying to St. Thomas and taking a ferry on to Tortola or Virgin Gorda. The ferry takes about one hour to Tortola and a bit longer to Virgin Gorda. It is a very pleasant trip.

Getting Ready

Entry Requirements

 A passport is required for entry into the BVI, but US and Canadian citizens may enter with a valid birth certificate, citizenship papers or voter's registration card plus a current photo ID. Visitors are asked to fill out a Tourist Information Card, half of which is collected when you pass through immigration and the other half as you depart. Luggage may be inspected. The departure tax is $10 for air travelers and $7 for those leaving on boats. No vaccinations are required.

US Customs

Items purchased in the BVI fall under the standard $600 per person duty-free allowance and can include one carton of cigarettes and one liter of alcohol. Items made on the islands (crafts, jewelry) are not subject to duty.

Canadian Customs

Canadian citizens can return with C$750 worth of merchandise if they have been out of the country seven days. The allowance is C$50 per day for a stay of under a week. The allowance can include one carton of cigarettes and 40 oz. of alcohol.

BVI Tourist Offices

The Tourist Office maintains a kiosk with good maps and brochures at the Road Town Ferry Dock. Hours are 10-4:30 weekdays. The main office, ☎ (284) 494-3134, is nearby on Wickham's Cay 1, just two blocks east of the Ferry Dock (same hours and virtually the same materials). The Virgin Gorda office is in the Yacht Harbour, in Spanish Town. Hours are 10-4:30 weekdays. ☎ (284) 495-5181.

In the US, the BVI maintain offices in New York, Atlanta and Los Angeles. The toll-free number is ☎ (800) 835-8530. Their website is www.bvitouristboard.com.

Money Matters

 US dollars are the currency in the BVI. Major credit cards are accepted at most hotels and upscale restaurants. There are still a few surprising exceptions, so do bring traveler's checks or cash. Traveler's checks are sometimes subject to a 10% stamp duty and so are American Express cards.

Many restaurants, particularly those in hotels, add a 10% service charge to your bill. Check whether it has been added before tipping. You can leave an additional amount if you choose. Tip as you would in the US.

Climate

 The weather here is lovely year-round and you can count on sunny days and cooler evenings. Temperatures are in the 70s and 80s in the winter. Daytime highs are in the 90s in the summer months.

The Caribbean hurricane season is late summer and early fall, but no hurricane has created havoc here in recent years.

Electric Current

Time Zone: The BVI are on Atlantic Standard Time.

US travelers need not bring adapters or converters, since current and sockets are identical to those on the US mainland.

Telephones

You can dial directly to the United States using your phone card or credit card. Or you can use ☎ 1-800 CALL USA (1-800-225-5872) using a credit card. You can also purchase a phone card at many retail or convenience stores. They must be used in special card phones, which are readily available.

You don't need to dial 284 for calls within the BVI, even when calling from one island to another.

The area code for the BVI is 284. The country code for the US and Canada is 1. Dial 1 plus the area code and number.

In a hotel, ask for the international operator. The hotel may add a small charge for the service.

Packing Tips

Whether you spend much of your vacation on a charter yacht or at a hotel, daytime attire will be very casual – pack lots of shorts, tank tops, T-shirts and sneakers and don't forget your bathing suits. It is acceptable to wear shorts and T-shirts in shops and restaurants in Road Town, but it is not polite to walk through town in a bathing suit!

Evening attire is also very casual. Be aware that guests at Little Dix Bay are requested to wear formal attire in the restaurant several evenings a week. Formal, in this case, means slacks and collared shirts for men (no ties) and any casually chic outfit for the ladies. The Sugar Mill restaurant at

Little Dix Bay is always informal. Guests at Peter Island Resort dress for dinner. You will feel more comfortable in casually smart attire at our upscale restaurants. There are many restaurants where you can dine in shorts, however.

- To prevent clothing from wrinkling in your suitcase, place tissue paper between the garments.

- Transparent zippered plastic bags, sold at five-and-dime stores, are ideal for carrying lingerie, cosmetics and shoes.

- Carry all liquids, shampoos, lotions and the like in plastic bottles. Breakage can ruin your clothes and luggage.

- Don't be a walking drugstore. Over the counter drugs and sundries are sold everywhere on the islands. Do, however, bring enough prescription drugs to last your entire trip, and be sure to bring your original prescription.

Holidays

January 1	New Year's Day
March	Commonwealth Day (changeable)
April	Easter Monday (changeable)
May or June	Whit Monday (changeable)
June	Sovereign's Birthday
August	Festival Monday, Tuesday and Wednesday
October 21	St. Ursula's Day
November	Birthday of Heir to the Throne
December 25	Christmas
December 26	Boxing Day

Sovereign's and Heir's Birthday are marked by lunches, dinners and flag-raising ceremonies at Government Building. Stores remain open.

Festival

 Usually held the first week in August, Festival (Carnival) is a lively time in the BVI. It is a way to celebrate the culture and heritage of the islanders and to mark the 1834 Slavery Emancipation Act. There is dancing to reggae bands at the fairgrounds and lots of booths serving typical Caribbean food and drink. Lots of partying too. A King and Queen are crowned on Tuesday and they lead a happy parade from the Prospect Reef Hotel into Road Town. There are horse races and lots of other competitions. All in good fun. Major events take place on Tortola, with mini-versions on Virgin Gorda and Jost Van Dyke.

Special Events

I'm sure it will not surprise you to find that many of the BVI's special events are water-oriented. There are yacht races virtually every month and boardsailing contests, fishing tournaments and even dinghy championships. On-land events include Festival, tennis tournaments and cycle races. There are often fish frys where local bands entertain and West Indian foods are served.

There are some annual events that are special. Contact the BVI tourist office for exact dates, ☎ 800-835-8530 or at www.bvitouristboard.com.

The **BVI Music Fest by the Sea** held in Tortola's Cane Garden Bay (usually the last weekend in May) is a three-day festival with musicians from the Caribbean, US, Europe and South Africa. There's a lot of reggae, some very good jazz, rhythm and blues and gospel. There are daytime events on the beach too. www.bvimusicfest.com.

The **BVI Spring Regatta and Sailing Festival** is the granddaddy of all races. Held in April, it is one leg of the Caribbean Ocean Racing Triangle (CORT), a series that begins months earlier in other parts of the Caribbean. Entrants gather at Nanny Cay on Tortola for the start of the race. Destinations ranging throughout the USVI, BVI and Puerto Rico are assigned for each race day. ☎ (284) 494-2322.

HIHO (Hook-in-Hold-on) is the major windsurfing (called boardsailing here) event. Held in June, it draws contestants from the USVI and Puerto Rico. The major events start on Tortola (Beef Island, Apple Bay or Josiah's Bay), but some events are on other islands. ☎ (284) 494-0337, www.hoho-bvi.com.

Foxy's Wooden Boat Regatta, held Memorial Day weekend on Jost Van Dyke, is over 30 years old and counting. It's a serious event, but all the activities connected with it make it a blast. ☎ (284) 495-9891.

Traditional Foods

 Although you can find restaurants that serve international cuisines, you will enjoy sampling some traditional West Indian foods during your stay. While some family-owned eateries serve the most authentic dishes, you'll find a sprinkling of tropical dishes on many menus. Another good way to sample traditional foods is to join in the fun at a typical West Indian barbeque, which is a weekly event at most hotels. Some island favorites include:

- **Roti** – Islanders favorite "fast food," rotis are flavorful East Indian flat breads filled with meat or vegetables. They resemble a wrap-sandwich and can be eaten while on the go.

- **Paté** – This is confusing because it is not like liver pâté, but rather refers to a pita-style bread that is filled with spiced meats, seafood or vegetables. The pate is baked or grilled and served warm.
- **Fungi (foongee)** – Made from corn-meal and ground vegetables (often okra), fungi is served as a side dish, primarily with seafood.
- **Whelks** – A seasonal seafood similar to escargot.
- **Conch (conk)** – Another local seafood favorite. Conch is served as an appetizer or entrée in soups, fritters and salads, or grilled.
- **Callaloo** – A thick soup of okra, ham, crabmeat and greens.
- **Curries and Stews** – Goat, mutton and chicken are often used to make curries and stews with local vegetables.
- **Local fruits** – Soursop is used to make ice cream. Guava, mango, pineapple, sugar apple, passion fruit and tamarind are delicious.

A Capsule History

 Christopher Columbus discovered the entire Virgin Island chain in 1493, but it was quickly forgotten. In 1595, Sir Francis Drake sailed into a

Introduction

serene channel (now named for him), formed by two large islands on the north and a series of smaller islands on the south strand. England laid claim to several of these islands, as did Spain and Holland. Island names such as Jost Van Dyke are Dutch, while Tortola (White Dove) and Virgin Gorda (Fat Virgin) are Spanish. In 1672, Tortola was annexed by England and made part of the Leeward Islands Government with Anguilla, St. Kitts and Nevis.

Privateers

Meanwhile, pirates discovered the islands, using the isolated cays and inlets to attack treasure-laden ships heading from South America to Europe. Robert Louis Stevenson used Norman Island as the setting for his novel *Treasure Island* and Dead Man's Chest was the site of a battle to the death for 15 privateers – all for a bottle of rum. At one point, privateers established a settlement at the West End of Tortola.

> Fifteen men on a dead man's chest
> Yo ho ho and a bottle of rum
> Drink and the devil had done for the rest
> Yo ho ho and a bottle of rum.
> The mate was fixed by the bosun's pike
> The bosun brained with a marlinspike
> And cookey's throat was marked belike
> It had been gripped by fingers ten;
> And there they lay, all good dead men
> Like break o'day in a boozing ken
> Yo ho ho and a bottle of rum.

Colonization & Slavery

English planters arrived and plantations were created. In the 18th century, a Quaker colony was established on Tortola and the planters and

Quakers joined forces to rid the islands of pirates. The sugar cane and cotton plantations required large numbers of slaves, which were brought from Africa. At one point, there were over 2,000 slaves on Virgin Gorda, almost equivalent to the entire population today. Slavery here was particularly cruel, but in 1807 when a planter beat his slave to death for eating a mango, public opinion galvanized against slavery. It was finally abolished in 1834. However, this served to destroy the islands' economy and today only remnants of once-elegant great houses remain. The land was parceled out and sold to former slaves, who started farming for their own use. These islands were extremely poor. Even tourism was late arriving here.

Tourism

In large measure, two men are responsible for the growth of tourism in the BVI. The first was **Laurence Rockefeller**, who built Little Dix Bay on Virgin Gorda, an island that did not have electricity, roads or a high school 30 years ago. The other, **Charlie Gary**, an avid sailor, turned his avocation into a multi-million dollar industry when he organized The Moorings Yacht Charters company with six boats in 1961.

The Islands Today

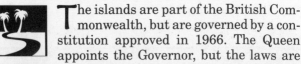 The islands are part of the British Commonwealth, but are governed by a constitution approved in 1966. The Queen appoints the Governor, but the laws are made and administered by a locally elected (every four years) chief minister and a popularly elected legislative council. As in the British system, the

chief minister is selected by the party that garners the most popular votes.

In 1966, Queen Elizabeth II visited here to approve the Constitution and to dedicate the Sir Francis Drake Highway, which runs from the West End to the East End of Tortola. She also officially opened the bridge connecting Tortola with Beef Island. The bridge is named for her. In 1977, Prince Charles visited.

Since 1984, when the British Virgin Islands adopted the "International Business Companies Legislation," over 210,000 companies have registered their businesses here. Most are banks with off-shore or private banking accounts, but there are also insurance and trust companies. While most British Virgin Islanders' work is connected to tourism, it is now only the second source of income for the government after banking.

Charter Yachts

 Charter yachting, once strictly the domain of the very rich, is the "in" vacation in the BVI. More than half the visitors to these islands spend part of their time aboard a yacht, which accounts for the huge number of yachts and the comparatively small number of hotel rooms available. There are two types of charters – bareboat and crewed.

Bareboat Charters

Overwhelmingly, bareboat charters, where no captain or crew are provided, are the choice here since it is this very idea that draws visitors to the BVI. There are innumerable coves and inlets for anchorages by day and night anchorages even offer good dining options. You can stay up all night or go to bed early, explore the Baths of Virgin Gorda on Monday and the caves of Norman Island on Tuesday. Provisioning is easy, so you can eat what you like, when you like, and all this in luxury. Most bareboat charterers operate as their own captain, with members of their party as crew.

Before you are permitted to charter a bareboat, you will be asked to furnish proof of your competence and cruising experience. You will need to complete a résumé detailing your boating background and testing your knowledge of anchoring and coastal navigation. If you can supply references from a sailing club, that will help. For your own safety, don't try to inflate your skills. If you are uncertain, arrange for a skilled captain to sail with you the first day or two.

Bareboat Charter Companies

The Moorings Ltd. is the largest charter company in the BVI and one of the largest in the Caribbean. They offer 32- to 50-foot monohulls and catamarans, which can be booked as bareboats or crewed. Mixed-stay packages available. In Road Town, Tortola. Write 19345 US Highway 19N, 4th floor, Clearwater, FL 33764. ☎ (800) 535-72890, www.moorings.com.

Horizon Yacht Charters offers their luxurious yachts fully equipped with linen, cooking utensils and a dinghy, as do most. Also, ASA sailing school gives lessons. Based at Nanny Cay Marina, Tortola. Write Box 3222 Road Town, Tortola, ☎ (284) 494-8787, www.horizonyachtcharters.com.

Barecat Charters has 35- to 50-foot yachts that are fully equipped and owner-operated should you desire a crew. Based at Frenchman's Cay Marina,

Soper's Hole, Tortola, ☎ (800) 296-5287, www.barecat.
com.

Sail Caribbean Yacht Charters' fleet has 50-foot
sloops outfitted with kayaks and scuba gear. They
are based at Hodge's Creek Marina, East of Road
Town. Write Box 3457, Road Town, ☎ (284)
495-1675, www.sailcaribbeanyachtcharters.com.

Bitter End Yacht Club is a luxurious resort on
North Sound, Tortola. It is the most popular venue
for mixed-stay packages and a real force in BVI
chartering. Write Box 46, Virgin Gorda, ☎ (800)
872-2392, www.beyc.com.

Euphoric Cruises at the Virgin Gorda Yacht Harbor has smaller boats, from 18- and 24-foot Robalos
and Makos to 28-foot Bertrams, ☎ (284) 495-5542,
www.boatsbvi.com.

Virgin Traders Motor Yachts specialize in motor
yachts rather than sailing vessels. They range in
size from 44 to 59 feet and are quite luxurious.
Bareboat or crewed. Based at Nanny Cay. Write Box
993, Road Town, Tortola, ☎ (284) 495-2526,
www.virgin-traders.com.

Crewed Charters

In this case you are renting a fully equipped yacht
with crew. Many bareboat charter operators rent the
bareboat and arrange for a professional crew. Dis-
cuss with the operator your itinerary, the size of
your party and any special needs you have. Crew
members are true professionals, usually with many
years of sailing experience. Once again, rates vary
with size, luxury and season.

Many charterboat operators who rent bareboats will
supply a captain and/or crew upon request. If you
charter a crewed yacht, it will be privately owned.

Crewed yachts are generally larger and have more creature comforts (like air conditioning, hot showers, gourmet food) and usually carry surfboards, snorkel and scuba gear and other watersports gear. In some cases, you can charter one stateroom rather than the entire boat. You then will sail with other guests.

Voyage Charters' fleet is comprised of specially built catamarans from South Africa. *Voyage 380, 440, 400* and *480* are built to be stable and fast. Each vessel has its own full-time crew aboard, including a skipper and chef. Based at Soper's Hole Marina, West End, Tortola. Write PO Box 3377, Annapolis, MD 21403, ☎ (888) 869-2436, www.voyagecharters.com.

Golden Spirit is a 46-foot power catamaran that can hold four guests. You can select the itinerary and the menus. Crewed only. Based at Fat Hog's Bay, East End, Tortola, ☎ (284) 499-2391, www.chartergoldenspirit.com.

Endless Summer II is a 72-foot ketch with four double staterooms. It carries watersports gear and the food is exceptional. Based at Nanny Cay. Write Box 823, Road Town, Tortola, ☎ (800) 368-9905, www.EndlessSummer.com.

Booking a Charter

If reading this section plants a seed in your mind, get information immediately. Arrangements should be made and confirmed long in advance of your arrival – often as far as one year ahead. This is particularly true if you want to charter during a major holiday or in high season. Rates are highest during holidays (when a minimum charter of one week is the norm) and from December 1 to April 30.

Mixed Stays (Hotel/Yacht)

A popular option is a combination hotel/yacht vacation. A typical package would offer three days
aboard a yacht and four days at the hotel. There are
longer stays available too. The package may include
a bareboat or crewed yacht. This is something to explore. These packages are primarily confined to the
summer months. Write to: Bitter End Yacht Club or
The Moorings (for addresses see pages 20-21).

Stocking Your Boat

Food and drinks (fuel too) are included in crewed
yacht rates and, unless you have some special needs,
you can rely on the captain. It is fun to arrange for
"split provisioning," which allows you to eat offshore. These meals are not included in your charter
fee.

If you intend to provision your own yacht, there are
many full provision stores. Major shops are found on
Tortola and Virgin Gorda.

BVI Anchorages

In order to sail in the area, you must have at your
fingertips detailed information on harbor entrances,
depths, reef locations and swell conditions. Your
charter operator offers the best source for this information.

Another good source, **Cruising Guides Publishers**, pub-
lish cruising guides and charts for BVI waters. Write Box
1017 Dunedin, FL 34697-1017, www.cruisingguides.com.

Some of the BVI ports of call have taken on legend-
ary status. They are real personality places and very
popular. Do call ahead to reserve. Below, a sampling
of anchorages (the actual number is astonishing):

Deadman's Bay is the perfect destination to get your sea legs under you. Just an hour or two sail from Road Town, it is part of Peter Island. You can eat dinner at the resort's restaurants and swim at Deadman's Beach.

Uninhabited **Norman Island** is the reputed setting of Robert Louis Stevenson's *Treasure Island*. You can hike a cattle track to the top of the island or have a drink at a floating restaurant.

Cooper Island has a lovely beach and the beach restaurant serves all three meals plus drinks. It's a good stop on the way to Virgin Gorda.

Virgin Gorda Baths are the most famous landmark in the BVI. Huge boulders form grottoes just right for snorkeling.

North Sound, Virgin Gorda is a stunning body of water that has several hotels with anchorage facilities. The sound is protected by surrounding islands such as Mosquito (Drake's Anchorage), Prickly Pear and Eustatia.

Trellis Bay, Beef Island is a busy stop and home to BVI Boardsailing School. The Cybernet Café and Da Loose Mongoose Bar are here too. On Bellamy Cay (in the bay), the Last Resort Restaurant is great fun (see pages 99 and 106).

Jost Van Dyke has three anchorages. **Little Harbour** has three restaurants and is quiet. **Great Harbour** has several West Indian restaurants, plus Foxy's Tamarind Bar. A tiny village, **White Bay**, is on the beach here.

Scuba Diving

Spearfishing is not allowed.

There are over 60 charted dive sites in the waters around the BVI and hundreds of reefs to snorkel, near islands and cays. The coral reefs are alive with colorful sponges and tropical fish.

The dive sites are extremely diverse, with pinnacles, drop-offs, ledges and caves. The most interesting dives are to wrecks of sunken ships, which abound in the area – 300 lie off Anegada alone.

Dive operators are experienced and well organized. Their equipment is first rate. They offer resort and introductory dive courses as well as PADI certification. They arrange to meet charter yachts for a dive and rent underwater cameras and all equipment.

Details about sites and operators are in the sections on *Scuba Diving* in the Tortola and Virgin Gorda chapters (pages 43 and 123).

National Parks

 The National Parks Trust was established in 1961 when the Rockefeller family made a gift of three sites to the BVI government. They were Sage Mountain on Tortola and Devil and Spring Bays on Virgin Gorda. On **Sage Mountain**, which is the highest point on any Virgin Island including the USVI, a reforestation effort began almost immediately. Vegetation was reintroduced that had disappeared from the island – so today's landscape is what Tortola may have looked like when Columbus first saw it in 1493. Even though the mountaintop gets only 100 inches of rain annually, the park resembles a tropical rainforest. Moisture is carried off the water by the winds as a fine mist.

Many of the elephant ear philodendrons, lacy ferns and white cedar trees have been brought together within the three-acre **Botanic Gardens** in Road Town. The gardens were created by the Trust and are maintained by volunteers. The plants are arranged according to habitat in sections reached by landscaped paths radiating from a three-tiered fountain.

The marine park, off Salt Island, is the **Rhone National Marine Park**, which is centered around the wreck of the *RMS Rhone* (see *Scuba Diving*, page 44). The park includes the wreck itself, two coral caves nearby and Dead Chest Island. The island's cliffs covered by cactus, sage and frangipani, are nesting sites for sea birds. There are also salt ponds rimmed by black mangrove trees.

Other parks include the bays on the southwest coast of Virgin Gorda, which are marked by huge granite boulders that have fallen in such a way as to create caves and underwater passages.

There are several sanctuaries on Anegada. One is for flamingos and the other for the endangered rock iguana. In order to protect the fragile reefs, the Trust has installed 180 mooring buoys at various anchorage areas.

Getting Married

Destination weddings, as they're called, have become increasingly popular and the BVI are a choice location. Weddings are easily arranged with little red tape. The easiest route is to contact the luxurious resorts such as Little Dix Bay (Virgin Gorda), Peter Island Resort and Long Bay Beach Hotel (Tortola). Traditional honeymoon destinations, they now offer wedding packages with many attractive amenities. Staff members work with you to make your wedding wonderful.

You can also make your own arrangements. You are required to be in the territory three days before you can be married. You can apply for the marriage license on the day you arrive. Below is a bare-bones description of what is involved.

- Go to the post office and purchase $110 in BVI stamps (Post Office is on Main Street, Road Town). This is the fee for your marriage license and this is the only way it can be paid.

- Apply for the license at the Attorney General's office, 2nd floor, Central Administration Complex on Wickham's Cay 1, Road Town. A valid passport stamped with your date of arrival in the BVI and showing proof of identity is required.

- Two witnesses are required at the wedding to sign the marriage certificate. If necessary two locals will do.

Once the valid license is issued after three business days, you have two options.

Civil ceremonies are conducted at the Registrar-General's office, also on Wickham's Cay. You should make arrangements when you apply for the license. Office hours are Mon-Fri 8:30 am-4:30 pm.

Weddings are performed in the office, Mon-Fri 9 am-4 pm, for $35. The registrar will also perform weddings on the beach or on a hillside, Mon-Sat 9 am-6:30 pm for a $100 fee. These fees can be paid by check. Once again, two witnesses are required.

If you prefer a **religious ceremony**, talk with the local minister. You can arrange for an in-church ceremony or one on a beach. Fees are negotiated, but the three-day requirement and license application still apply.

There are wedding planners and photographers available. Check www. intheislands. com for more information.

There are Roman Catholic churches and churches of many Protestant denominations. The BVI Tourist Board can help you find the church of your faith. We are not aware of any synagogues or mosques in the BVI.

For up-to-the-minute details contact:
Registrar's Office
Box 418
Road Town, Tortola BVI
☎ (284) 494-3492

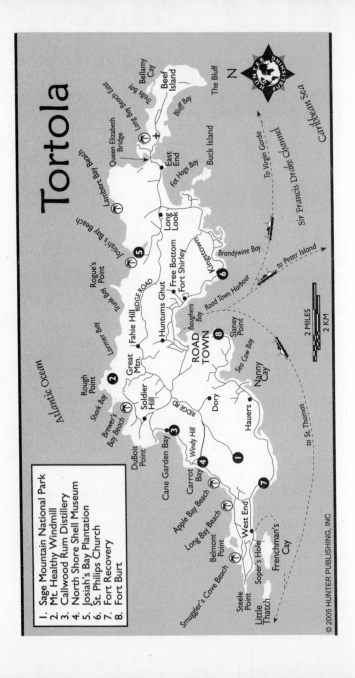

Tortola

1. Sage Mountain National Park
2. Mt. Healthy Windmill
3. Callwood Rum Distillery
4. North Shore Shell Museum
5. Josiah's Bay Plantation
6. St. Philips Church
7. Fort Recovery
8. Fort Burt

© 2005 HUNTER PUBLISHING, INC

Atlantic Ocean

Caribbean Sea

Sir Francis Drake Channel

To Virgin Gorda

to Peter Island

to St. Thomas

ROAD TOWN

Road Town Harbour

West End

Soper's Hole

Little Thatch

Frenchman's Cay

Steele Point

Smuggler's Cove Beach

Belmont Point

Long Bay Beach

Apple Bay Beach

Cane Garden Bay

DuBois Point

Brewer's Bay Beach

Shark Bay

Rough Point

Great Mtn.

Soldier Hill

Windy Hill

Carrot Bay

Dory

Hauers

Nanny Cay

Sea Cow Bay

Slaney Point

Boughers Bay

Fahie Hill

Huntums Ghut

Free Bottom

Fort Shirley

RIDGE ROAD

RIDGE RD

Lamber Bay

Rogue's Point

Trunk Bay Point

Lorner Bay

Josiah's Bay Beach

Long Look

Brandywine Bay

Kingstown

Queen Elizabeth Bridge

East End

Fat Hogs Bay

Buck Island

Buck Island

Long Bay Beach East

Lambert Bay

Trellis Bay

Bluff Bay

Bellamy Cay

Beef Island

The Bluff

2 MILES

2 KM

N

Tortola

Tortola, which means "turtledove" in Spanish, is the principal island of the British Virgin Islands. It is home to some 16,000 people, a fourth of whom live in the picturesque capital, Road Town. The island, only 12 miles long and three miles wide, could easily be circled by car in just a few hours if it weren't for the mountain chain that splits its core. The jagged peaks create beautiful vistas, as well as breathtaking hairpin turns and extremely steep grades. These will slow you down a bit and allow you to really explore Tortola.

An attractive island, Tortola is surprisingly rural and slow-paced. There is no industry and the only agricultural development visible are small private gardens. Most goods, including foodstuffs, are imported.

There are only a handful of roads and these meander along the shores, passing small villages, private homes, churches of various persuasions, grocery stores, laundromats, groups of wandering goats, lambs and an occasional cow.

The southern coast, which fronts the Sir Francis Drake Channel, is more developed, with lots of cays, islets and coves. The island's best marinas are here, as is Road Town. It is drier and not nearly as flowered as the northern coast. All the beautiful beaches are on the northern coast and they stretch for miles. Cane Garden Bay Beach is very popular, but Long Bay and Apple Bay Beaches are my personal favorites. Fruit trees, palms and seagrapes dot the beach strips and line the two-lane road.

Tortola's hotels are an eclectic group, with some at the shore, others on mountaintops in sugar mills and ancient forts. The island has a surprising num-

There are no US-style fast food outlets here.

ber of good dining options that run the gamut from gourmet to fast food. A favorite West Indian fast food are "rotis," which are rather like wraps.

Whether you spend most of your vacation time aboard ship or on land, Tortola is relaxed, low-key and informal. It is friendly and hospitable as well.

Getting There

By Air

There are no direct flights to Tortola from the US or Canada. Because Beef Island Airport can handle only commuter-size planes, most visitors fly via a major carrier into San Juan, Puerto Rico or St. Thomas, US Virgin Islands, then transfer to smaller aircraft for the short flight from there (40 minutes from San Juan; 20 minutes from St. Thomas). **American Eagle**, **Liat**, **Air Sunshine** and **Cape Air** all have daily flights between San Juan and Tortola. All except American Eagle have daily flights from St. Thomas as well. Make these reservations at the same time as making your direct flight, for the small planes fill up quickly. Check bags only to your initial stop. When you get there, recheck them with the local carrier. Delayed baggage is endemic here.

Airlines Serving the Caribbean		
American/ American Eagle	☎ 800-433-7300	www.aa.com
Air Sunshine	☎ 800-327-8900	www.airsunshine.com
Cape Air	☎ 800-352-0714	www.flycapeair.com

Continental Airlines	☎ 800-523-3273	www.continental.com
Delta Airlines	☎ 800-221-1212	www.delta.com
Jet Blue	☎ 800-538-2583	www.jetblue.com
Liat	☎ 868-624-4727	www.liatairline.com
US Airways	☎ 800-428-4322	www.usairways.com

Note: Tortola's airport is on Beef Island – just 300 feet off Tortola's eastern tip and reached by crossing the Queen Elizabeth II Bridge (toll 50¢). It is 20 minutes from Road Town.

Tortola

By Sea

St. Thomas - Tortola

Several ferry lines connect Charlotte Amalie, St. Thomas and Tortola. Large and comfortable (some have sundecks), they take one hour to Tortola's West End Ferry Dock and 15 minutes more to Road Town. Not every ferry continues on to Road Town. There are also ferries from Red Hook, St. Thomas. These take half an hour. At this writing the round-trip fare is $45. Taxis meet each ferry.

Tip: Don't forget you need a passport or proof of citizenship plus a photo ID.

The schedules below are accurate at this writing. They do change, however, so check before making plans.

Smith's Ferry Services, ☎ (340) 775-7292 on St. Thomas and (284) 495-4495 on Tortola.

Return ferries take longer because they make a stop in St. John for immigration and customs inspections.

Native Son Inc, ☎ (340) 774-8685 on St. Thomas and (284) 495-4617 on Tortola.

These two companies alternate schedules so there is always a ferry available.

From Charlotte Amalie

Monday-Friday: 8:25 am, 8:55, 12:15 pm, 12:45, 1:30, 2, 2:30, 4:30, 5
Saturday: 8:25 am, noon, 12:30 pm, 1:30, 2, 2:30, 4:45
Sunday: 8 am, 8:30, 10:45, 1:45 pm, 2:45 and 5:30

From Red Hook

Daily: 7:45 am, 8, 11:15, 2:55 pm, 3:15, 5, 5:30

St. John - Tortola

Inter-Island Boat Services, ☎ (240) 776-6597 on St. John and (284) 495-4166 on Tortola, has service between Cruz Bay and West End, Tortola. Daily service at 8:30 am, 11:30, 3:30 pm (except Sunday), 5 (Friday only). Return ferry at 9:15 am, 12:15 pm, 4:15 (except Sunday), 5:15 pm (Friday only).

Inter-Island Travel

Ferries connect Tortola to Virgin Gorda, Peter Island and Jost Van Dyke several times each day. The other islands require special arrangements with water taxis or can be visited on day trips.

By Sea

Tortola - Virgin Gorda

Two lines operate between Road Town and the St. Thomas Bay Jetty in the Valley, Virgin Gorda.

Smith's Ferry Service, ☎ (284) 495-4495, runs four ferries daily, Monday through Saturday, and three ferries on Sunday. Some early morning ferries continue on to St. John and St. Thomas after stopping in Road Town. The trip takes 30 minutes and costs $35 to St. John or $40 to St. Thomas.

Speedy's, ☎ (284) 495-5240, based on Virgin Gorda, has five ferries daily, Monday through Saturday, and three ferries on Sunday. Ferries continue on to St. John and St. Thomas on Tuesdays, Thursdays and Saturdays. Rates are the same as Smith's, above.

North Sound (Virgin Gorda)

The **North Sound Express** connects Beef Island with Spanish Town and then the Bitter End Yacht Club six times daily. North Sound Peninsula, an area that is not accessible by road, is home to the Bitter End, Biras Creek Resort and Leverick Bay Resort as well. Check in at the ferry desk on Beef Island. The boat is 36 feet long, totally enclosed and really flies. Reservations are essential.

The terminal point is the Bitter End Yacht Club and small boats from Saba Rock Island, Biras Creek and Leverick Bay meet the ferry, ☎ (284) 495-2138.

Tortola - Peter Island

Free to guests of the resort or those with dining reservations ($15 roundtrip for non-guests), the ferry runs from 7 am to 10:30 pm daily. The ride takes 20 minutes. This is a terrific day trip for Tortola-based visitors. It leaves from the Peter Island ferry dock, east of town. Many natives refer to this dock as the CSY (Caribbean Sailing Yacht) Dock because that's what it was for many years. For exact schedules, ☎ (284) 495-2000.

Leverick Bay Resort can be reached by car as well.

Tortola - Jost Van Dyke

Jost Van Dyke Ferry Service, ☎ (284) 494-2997, has regularly scheduled service between West End and Jost Van Dyke. There are six ferries from Monday through Friday and four on Sunday. Their last return ferry leaves Jost Van Dyke at 5 pm. That doesn't allow you to party at Foxy's unless you stay over or get a water taxi.

New Horizon Ferry Service, ☎ (284) 495-9278, also has service from West End. They have five ferries from Monday through Friday but only four on Saturday and Sunday. Their last return ferry is at 4:40 pm.

Tortola - Marina Cay

A ferry leaves from Trellis Bay on Beef Island virtually every hour from 10 am to 7 pm. Dinner guests will be met and returned on a private run, ☎ (284) 494-2174.

By Air

Tortola - Anegada

There's a flight from Beef Island on Monday, Wednesday, Friday and Sunday with **Clair Aero Services**, ☎ (284) 495-2271.

> **Note:** You will have to show your passport and go through a perfunctory customs check whether you arrive by air or by ferry.

Getting Around

Since there is no public transportation on Tortola, you will have to rely on taxis or rent a car or jeep.

Taxis

Your hotel can call a taxi for you and there are several taxi stands around the island. The main stand is at the Road Town ferry dock, ☎ (284) 494-3456. At Nanny Cay, call ☎ (284) 494-0539; at West End, ☎ (284) 495-4934. Most taxis, which meet flights and ferries, are vans or open-sided trucks. There are no published rates so you should set the fare in advance with the driver. The charge is for the taxi and not per person. Taxis also do sightseeing tours. Expect to pay about $20 per hour, but you negotiate the price with the driver.

Car/Jeep Rentals

We urge you to rent a car for at least part of your stay here. This will give you time to explore the island at your own pace and return to those spots you enjoy most whenever you wish. Hotels and restaurants are scattered through the island; you cannot walk from one to the other, except for those in Road Town.

To rent a car, you must be 21 years of age and hold a valid driver's license. You will be issued a temporary BVI license, good for 90 days, for a fee of $10. There are several car rental firms on Tortola, but none has facilities at the airport. Rates vary with season and type of car you require, but are generally a bit higher

Tortola

than those on the mainland. Virtually all the agencies below rent both cars and jeeps.

Avis, near the Botanic Gardens, ☎ (284) 494-3322.

Dollar Rent A Car, Prospect Reef & Long Bay Resort, ☎ (284) 494-6093.

Hertz, West End Dock & Wickham's Cay, ☎ (284) 495-4405.

D&D Car Rentals, Road Town & West End, ☎ (284) 495-4765.

ITGO Car Rentals, Wickham's Cay I, ☎ (284) 494-5150.

All have pick-up service at hotels.

Driving Tips

Roads are not marked with route numbers but there are signs to indicate directions and sites.

Driving here is on the left side of the road, as it is in the USVI. There are very few roads and no traffic lights on the island. Roads are two lanes and paved. Most areas are well-maintained, although often cracks are visible.

There is one road (going east to west) along the north shore and another (**Waterfront Drive**) along the south shore. A handful of roads cross the mountain range and these are marked by steep ascents and descents with hairpin turns that can take your breath away. **Ridge Road** travels east to west on the mountain range in mid-island and also has hairpin turns.

The 35 mph speed limit drops to 20 mph in residential areas. These are marked by speed bumps.

Relax, take a deep breath and blow your horn to alert oncoming traffic. You'll soon feel like a pro. Even if you take the wrong turn and end up at your starting point, as I have done innumerable times, you'll have great views of Road Town and other parts of the island. Pick up a map at the rental agency or the tourist kiosk.

Drivers are polite, but tailgating is common and cars often pass in unexpected spots. Anyone who lives in a large US city will not even notice.

Bicycle Rentals

Last Stop Sports at Nanny Cay rents bikes for adults and children. Delivery to your hotel, ☎ (284) 494-0564.

Orientation

Tortola, the largest island in the British Virgin Islands, is home to 16,000 people, most of whom live in the capital, Road Town. Tortola and adjacent Beef Island form the northern strand of islands on The Sir Francis Drake Channel. Tortola is the hub of the BVI and is the best kick-off point for day trips to Virgin Gorda, Peter Island and the nearby US Virgin Islands, St. John and St. Thomas.

Tortola

Over 80% of BVI residents live on Tortola.

Road Town

Although it is the capital and administrative center of the British Virgin Islands, Road Town is tiny even by Caribbean standards. It was originally called Road Harbor, which was appropriate, since its huge harbor, home to several marinas, is the hub of the island. A really picturesque town, it has two main streets – Sir Francis Drake Highway (called Waterfront Drive) and Main Street.

Waterfront Drive hugs the harbor and houses the BVI Tourist Board, customs and immigration facilities, several shops and restaurants. As this road leaves the harbor area, it heads east along the shore to Beef Island or west along the shore to the

West End ferry dock. Look for Pusser's Co. Store and Pub here.

Main Street, the second street from the harbor, is quite long and winding. The town runs from Government House and the hospital on the west (left facing town) to the Botanical Gardens and police station on the east. En route you'll find the post office, the old prison, the courthouse, many shops and restaurants.

A wooden planter that serves as a traffic circle marks one entrance to **Wickham's Cay I**, which extends into the harbor. On this cay, you'll find several of our favorite restaurants, lots of shops (including three small shopping centers) and the **Village Cay Marina**. Wickham's Cay I is an integral part of town and easy to reach.

Moving eastward from town, passing the island's cultural center and the Treasure Isle Hotel, **Wickham's Cay II** is a mini-village built around a marina. Here, you'll find **The Moorings**, the largest charter operator in the Caribbean.

Around Tortola

A marina and hotel complex on the island's southern shore, **Nanny Cay** lies midway between Road Town and West End.

A small island near West End, **Frenchman's Cay** is connected to the mainland by a small bridge. Pusser's Landing Restaurant is located here, as is a fine anchorage called **Soper's Hole**.

Literally at the western edge of Tortola, **West End**, with a general store and the Jolly Roger Bar, is where most ferries dock. Customs is located here.

Cane Garden Bay, Tortola (Werner J. Bertsh, Voyages Ariane Travel)

Above: Marina Cay, Tortola (Jim Scheiner, Voyages Ariane Travel)

Below: Hobie Cats racing off Tortola (www.britishvirginislands.de)

Above: Tortola beach (http://128.226.37.29/tortola)

Below: Scuba sights, Tortola (www.securenet.net/members/bporter/bvi)

Above: Scuba sights, Tortola (www.securenet.net/members/bporter/bvi)

Below: On the reefs, Tortola (www.securenet.net/members/bporter/bvi)

Above: Little Dix Bay, Virgin Gorda

Below: Dining terrace, Little Dix Bay

The Baths, Virgin Gorda (Jim Scheiner, Voyages Ariane Travel)

Apply Bay has strong waves for surfers, is on the island's north shore and has an informal hotel and restaurant. **Long Bay** is nearby.

Cane Garden Bay is the hub of the island's north shore, has a number of restaurants, and is a watersports center. Palm trees line the long stretch of beach here.

Sage Mountain National Park is the highest point on the island, at 1,800 feet. This is a 92-acre mountain reserve, which has a primeval rainforest.

The drive from Road Town on the island's East End follows the hilly shore, passing beautiful bays and several residential areas. From East End you can cross the Queen Elizabeth Bridge to **Beef Island**, where the airport is located.

From Sunup to Sundown

The sun, the sea, and the sand are the key attractions, as they are throughout the Caribbean. If those are what you are looking for, then you'll think the British Virgin Islands are top notch. The weather is as good as it comes, with days invariably warm and sunny. The ever-present trade winds keep the temperatures moderate (for the Caribbean) and keep the scores of sailing ships moving from one anchorage to the next throughout the year.

While Tortolians have a laissez-faire attitude toward life in general, they are very disciplined and extremely well-organized about the active sports that take place in the waters around these islands – inhabited and uninhabited alike. Certainly yacht charters are the most popular type of vacation here and it is true that half of the visitors to the BVI are aboard yachts for at least part of their vacations.

But chartering is not everyone's cup of tea. Scuba diving is also first rate and, with 60 dive sites in the area, you can indulge yourself in this exciting pursuit. Day-sails whisk you to uninhabited islands, where you can snorkel over virgin reefs. There is windsurfing, waterskiing, sport fishing and sailing schools.

Landlubbers can have a delightful time sunning and shelling on one of Tortola's north shore beaches; hike through Sage Mountain National Park; go horseback riding; play nine holes at a seaside pitch n' putt; play tennis; or tour a rum distillery that makes rum the old-fashioned way.

> **Note:** Jet-skis, which are very popular in the US and on many Caribbean Islands, are not permitted here. They kick up sand from the ocean floor that damages the reefs.

Frequent ferry service between Tortola and Virgin Gorda, Peter Island and Jost Van Dyke makes it easy to hop one for an enjoyable day spent exploring another island.

Of course, if your idea of a wonderful vacation is a comfortable lounge under a swaying palm with a nail-biting P.D. James mystery in one hand and a banana daiquiri in the other, that's OK too. No hard sell here.

Let's start with the sea and sand.

Beaches

 Tortola's beaches are located on the island's northern shore across the mountain chain from Road Town. They are less developed than those on many Caribbean Islands and have thick white sand, palm and seagrape trees and crys-

tal-clear blue water. They are rarely crowded. Facilities run the gamut from none to beach shacks and watersports centers to resort hotels with lovely beachfront restaurants. Cane Garden Bay is the most developed and is most crowded on weekends. We'll suggest some places to pick up a picnic lunch. The following are listed in order from West End to East End.

Smuggler's Cove

The beach at Tortola's West End is at the end of Belmont Road. It's stunning, with calm bright blue waters that are quite warm due to the currents. Snorkeling is terrific here and there is a marked underwater trail. An honor bar offers beer, soda and munchies. Put your money in the cigar box and help yourself. Belmont Road is dirt, pot-holed, rock-strewn and a chiropractor's dream. It's about 10 very bumpy minutes from Long Bay Beach. Four-wheel drive is a plus but not a must.

Long Bay Beach West

A personal favorite, this mile-long strip of sandy beach fronts the **Long Bay Beach Hotel**. You can rent watersports gear and lounge chairs and eat at the poolside restaurant. The beach is so long that the western end is rather isolated. The waters here are rougher than those at Smuggler's Cove, but still great for swimming and watersports.

Apple Bay Beach

Another long stretch of white sand, this bay fronts the informal **Sebastian's Hotel**. This is a great beach for surfing, particularly during the winter months. Sebastian's rents windsurf boards, snorkel equipment, lounges and beach tennis gear. There is a restaurant and bar.

Cane Garden Bay Beach

The island's most popular beach, Cane Garden Bay is studded with palm trees for shade. The sand here is packed down and not as luxurious as Long Bay and Apple Bay. There is always a lot of activity for there are several locally owned restaurants and bars nearby. **Rhymer's Beach Shack** rents all sorts of sports gear and its restaurant is a popular spot. Stick around for one of Cane Garden Bay's special sunsets. Salute it with a drink at **Stanley's Welcome Bar**. Look for the tire swing.

Brewer's Bay

There is a basic tent campground where, except at the height of the season, you'll be virtually alone. There is a fine reef offshore but no rental facility, so bring gear with you. There is a commissary, but you are better off bringing lunch. Showers.

Josiah's Bay

Isolated on Tortola's northeast coast, which is its least developed area, this beach has an unusual rock formation at one end. The sand strip is long and wide and great for sunbathing. There is a small beach bar and **The Secret Garden Restaurant** nearby is great for take-out. In the winter, this is a great surfing beach. The road to the beach is rough and you'd do best with four-wheel drive.

Lambert Bay

Also known as Elizabeth Bay, this area has the **Lambert Bay Resort** behind the sand strip. The beach is studded with palm trees and has fine white sand. Access is through a private road, not from the hotel. There is a poolside snack shop.

Long Bay East

On the island's north shore and just off the tip of Tortola, this is a shell-filled beach that has a marked underwater snorkel trail.

Scuba Diving

There are over 60 charted dive sites in BVI waters and diving is exceptional. Options range from remote offshore pinnacles to lush coral gardens and fantastic shipwrecks. No two dives are alike and each has a unique attraction. Most of the diving is done near the islands and rocks that line the Sir Francis Drake Channel. Their rather isolated locations assure superior visibility and healthy coral. No matter what the weather there are always calm protected places to dive and because there are so many sites, you may end up at one all by yourself.

The depths – from 20-80 feet – are moderate and some sites are fine for snorkelers as well as divers. Others are spectacular, over sea mounts laced with dramatic edges and undercuts. The reefs are alive with sponges and schools of fish. It is not unusual to see tarpon, amberjack, sharks and turtles. The best wreck dive in the Caribbean is in BVI waters. The RMS *Rhone* (see below) sank off Salt Island in 1867 and has settled in 75 feet of water.

Legend has it that there are over 300 wooden ships at the bottom of the sea near Anegada.

Dive centers are independently owned and operated. They frequently have multiple locations including major hotels. Dive boats are generally large, seaworthy and uncrowded. The guides are familiar with the sites and the creatures in them.

Tortola

If you aren't certified, this could be a great opportunity to fix the problem since the schools here offer first-rate PADI and NAUI courses and also introductory resort courses.

Best Dive Sites

Wreck of the RMS Rhone

This is the BVI's premier dive. Anchored off Peter Island to take on cargo when a hurricane struck, the *Rhone*, a 310-foot British mail and passenger steamer, tried to maneuver through the storm. It foundered off Salt Island, broke in two and sank on October 28, 1867. Today her remains are well preserved. The bow rests in 75 feet of water and the stern is scattered from 15-50 feet. The ship's foremast, complete with crow's nest, the engine and battered propeller, are home to coral and beautiful fish. The *Rhone* was featured in a movie, *The Deep*, but despite the fact that the movie was terrible it served to stimulate interest in diving in the BVI.

The Indians

This is one of the sites that both divers and snorkelers can enjoy. Not far from Norman Island, four large pinnacles resembling Indian chiefs protrude from the surface of the water. Rising 90 feet from the ocean floor, these jagged structures form a series of "playgrounds" for marine creatures and coral.

The Chikuzen

Experienced divers will enjoy diving to this ship that was scuttled in 1981. In the open sea, a few miles from Beef Island, this Japanese refrigeration ship lies on its side in 75 feet of water. The 246-foot hulk has become home to thousands of fish, as well as octopus and barracudas.

The Chimneys

Located west of Great Dog Island are a series of coral channels and submarine arches. A winding canyon leads to a unique underwater arch. Colorful soft sponges and coral line the walls and fish glide through the coral garden.

Painted Walls & Blonde Rock

Painted Walls, a shallow dive off the southern point of Dead Chest Island is just right for inexperienced divers. The colorful coral and sponges are encrusted on the walls of four long gullies and most of the dive is in 20-30 feet of water. Painted Walls is usually visited in conjunction with Blonde Rock, which is a pinnacle between Dead Chest and Salt Island. Its rock, ledges, tunnels and caves are inhabited by crabs, lobsters, reef fish and fan corals.

Alice in Wonderland

This exciting dive is in South Bay off Ginger Island. The wall slopes gently downward from a depth of 15 feet to over 100 feet. Huge mushroom-shaped corals give the site its name.

Anegada

Unique in the Virgin Islands, Anegada is a flat coral island, while all the others are volcanic in origin. Surrounding the island is a massive fringing reef, which has claimed over 300 ships. Fish, coral and sponges are everywhere.

Do not try to sail here on your own. The reef is dangerous.

> **Note:** Many mooring sites are protected by the National Park's Trust. AA valid permit is required. The Park's Office in Road Town issues them as do the charter yacht companies. ☎ (284) 494-3904.

Dive Operators

Aquaventure Scuba Services, Village Cay, Road Town, ☎ (284) 494-4320, www.aquaventurebvi.com. Dives and PADI Resort course.

Blue Water Divers, Nanny Cay & Soper's Hole, West End, ☎ (284) 494-2847, www.ultimatebvi.com/ bluewater. Dives, resort course, equipment rentals, rendezvous service.

Underwater Safaris, Mooring's Dock, Road Town, ☎ (284) 494-3235, www.underwatersafaris.com. Dives, resort course, night dives, hotel/dive and sail packages.

Trimarine *Cuan Law*, Box 3069, Road Town, ☎ (800) 648-3393 or (284) 494-2490, www.bvidiving. com. This is a different diving experience. You live on a crewed 105-foot yacht for a week, moving from one dive site to another. All skill levels acceptable. The yacht holds 18 passengers and is bookable by individuals as well as groups.

Rainbow Visions Photo Center, Box 680, Road Town, ☎ (284) 494-2794, www.rainbowvisionbvi.com. Underwater photography and custom videos. Instruction, rentals. Office is at Prospect Reef Resort.

Snorkeling & Day-Sails

You don't have to be a diver to take in the underwater world of coral formations and exotic plant and marine life. Even novice snorkelers can enjoy the experience because the waters are so clear and the arrangement of the islands provides protection from wind and currents. Snorkeling is suitable for all ages from children to grandparents and it does not require heavy gear. Many people bring their own snorkel gear but you can easily rent it at your hotel's watersports center and the rental shacks on Cane Garden Bay Beach.

On Tortola, one of the most popular snorkel spots is **Smuggler's Cove** at the island's West End. It's a beautiful u-shaped cove with lovely white sand and a reef that extends from the shoreline for several hundred yards. **Long Bay East** (Beef Island), **Brewer's Beach** and **Cane Garden Bay Beach** also have reefs not far from shore.

Bring a hat, towel and sunscreen.

While these reefs are fun, they are not as exciting as the reefs at nearby islands and snorkel areas. If you rent a boat, some suggestions follow but, if not, consider joining a half- or full-day sailing trip to enjoy both the above and below water sights. Similar trips are available on powerboats. These trips usually include snorkel gear, lunch and an open bar.

Tortola

Special Snorkeling Areas

The Baths and **Devil's Bay**, Virgin Gorda, are the single most popular snorkel areas in the BVI. Tropical fish live in the tunnels and crevices formed by enormous granite boulders. You can snorkel from one to the other.

The **Norman Island Caves** are home to friendly yellow tails and sargeant majors. The caves shimmer with orange cup coral and red covering sponge. Also near Norman Island, **Benures Bay** on the northeastern shore has a shallow reef good for novices. Here you'll see parrotfish, yellowtail, octopus and small barracudas.

Green Cay and **Sandy Spit** near Little Jost Van Dyke have a reef that is a popular spot for cruising yachts.

White Bay on Peter Island has a long shallow reef with small-mouthed grunts, tarpon and octopus.

Some Reliable Day-Sail Companies

*Day sails
cost about
$75 per day.*

White Squall II, Box 145, Road Town, ☎ (284) 494-2564, www.whitesquall2.com.

A magnificent 80-foot schooner, *White Squall* has been plying these waters for many years. Destinations vary from The Baths (Virgin Gorda) to Cooper Island and to Norman Island. Snorkel gear, barbecue lunch, complimentary drinks included. Based at Village Cay Marina, Road Town.

Patouche Charters, Box 987, Road Town, ☎ (284) 494-6300, www.patouche.com.

Patouche owns two schooners. The larger heads to Norman Island, Peter Island and The Indians, while the smaller sails to Scrub Island, Virgin Gorda and Salt Island. Full-day trips include lunch, beverages and snorkel gear. Leaves from Penn's Marina, Fat Hog's Bay, East End.

Blue Ocean Adventures, Prospect Reef Resort, Box 437, Road Town, ☎ (284) 494-2872, www.blueoceanbvi.com. Owns the *Cat Ppalu*, a 75-foot catamaran, one of the largest and fastest day-sailing yachts in the BVI. It offers snorkel trips, sunset cruises and visits to nearby islands. Leaves from Prospect Reef Marina, Road Town.

Aristocat Charters, General Delivery, West End, ☎ (284) 495-4087, www.aristocatcharters.com. The *Aristocat* is a 48-foot catamaran. It holds only 14 people so it's a good choice for families. They often go to Pelican and Peter Island. Lunch, drinks and gear are included. Full-day, half-day and sunset cruises.

Kuralu, Soper's Hole Marina, Box 609, West End, ☎ (284) 495-4381, www.kuralu.com. With its red, white and blue sail, this 50-foot luxurious catamaran sets sail for Jost Van Dyke, Norman and Peter

Island with a small group. It is a safe choice for children. Lunch, drinks and snorkel gear are included.

Powerboat Companies

Tamarin Charters, Box 3069, Village Cay, Road Town, ☎ (284) 495-9837, www.tamarincharters.com. The *Tamarin II* is a 55-foot trimaran. Its destinations include The Caves at Norman Island, The Baths at Virgin Gorda and even Anegada. Full-day and half-day trips have multiple snorkel stops. Lunch is included on full-day trips. The *Tamarin III* is a 27-foot power cat. It goes on fun two-hour cruises and half-day snorkel trips.

Jolly Mon Charters, Box 471, Maya Cove, East End, ☎ (284) 495-9916, jollymon@surfbvi.com. Powerboat rentals, island hopping and snorkel trips. Fishing trips too.

Windsurfing (Boardsailing)

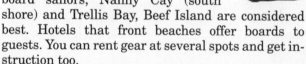

Windsurfing, called boardsailing here, is a popular sport and one taken very seriously as monthly regattas can confirm. Some of the races island-hop, but you'll probably do best sticking to a single bay. For advanced board sailors, Nanny Cay (south shore) and Trellis Bay, Beef Island are considered best. Hotels that front beaches offer boards to guests. You can rent gear at several spots and get instruction too.

Rental Companies

Boardsailing, BVI, Box 537, Trellis Bay, Beef Island, rents boards and gives two-hour lessons. They offer clinics for beginners, intermediates and advanced surfers. They also rent single and double

Some companies will deliver the board to your hotel.

Tortola

kayaks, surfboards and Hobie Cats. Their office is at the Trellis Bay Cybercafe, ☎ (284) 495-2447, www.windsurfing.vi.

HIHO, Box 857, Road Town (on Wickham's Cay I), is another rental company that offers instruction. The shop fronts the Sir Francis Drake Channel, ☎ (284) 494-0337, www.go-hiho.com.

Last Stop Sports, Box 3208, Road Town, ☎ (284) 494-0564, is strictly a rental agency but, since their headquarters is at Nanny Cay, it's very popular. They also rent kayaks, surfboards and body boards. They deliver to your hotel.

Water-Skiing, Surfing & Parasailing

It's not as popular as windsurfing, but a few places offer water-skiing. **Cane Garden Bay Pleasure Boats** on Cane Garden Bay is one, ☎ (284) 495-9660, and **Last Stop Sports** at Nanny Cay is another, ☎ (284) 494-0564. If you rent a powerboat you can add on water-ski equipment. Half-day and full-day rentals are available at **Sail Caribbean**, Hodges Creek Marina, East End, ☎ (284) 495-1675.

You won't find gigantic Hawaiian-style waves on Tortola, but you can "hang-10," particularly in the winter months. **Apple Bay** in front of Sebastian's Hotel (North Shore Road) is most popular with young Tortolians. **Josiah's Bay** is often fine as well, but it is not as easy to get to.

Want to see the channel from above? **Parasail, BVI** is your only option on Tortola. You take off and land on a boat driven by a US Coast Guard-licensed captain. Their office is at Soper's Hole, West End, ☎ (284) 495-4967.

Sailing Schools

Learn to sail on your vacation! Live aboard a crewed yacht and take a weeklong "Learn to Sail" course. It includes both on-water and classroom instruction. Beginners and Advanced Classes and Certification are offered. Contact:

Costs depend on the season and class. Check the websites for details.

- **Offshore Sailing School**, ☎ (800) 221-4326, www.offshore-sailing.com.
- **Full Sail Sailing School**, ☎ (284) 494-0512, www.fullsailbvi.com.
- **Sail Caribbean Sailing School**, ☎ (284) 495-1675, www.sailcaribbean.com.

Sport Fishing

Tournaments draw competitors from all parts of the world. They are fishing for blue marlin, wahoo, swordfish, shark, king fish and tuna. Under BVI rules, the captain keeps the catch, but he usually allows several fish to go back to the hotel with you.

Blue marlin are most prevalent in May, June and July.

Caribbean Fly Fishing, ☎ (284) 494-4797, caribbeanflyfishing@surfbvi.com.

Persistence Charters, ☎ (284) 495-4122.

Grand Slam Fishing, ☎ (284) 494-1535.

Island Boyz, ☎ (284) 495-6168, islandboyz@surfbvi.com.

Short-Term Boat Rentals

Cane Garden Bay Pleasure Boats on Cane Garden Bay rents power-boats with bimini-tops for shade, full safety equipment and ship-to-shore radios. You can rent for a half-day, full day or by the week. They also rent Hobie Cats, Sunfish, kayaks, windsurf boards, canoes and snorkeling gear, ☎ (284) 495-9660.

Sail Caribbean at Hodges Green Marina, East End is a multifaceted operation that rents kayaks, ocean floats, dinghies and scuba equipment. They give scuba diving instruction and offer dive packages. They also run a fine sailing school (see above), ☎ (284) 495-2447.

Golf

 There is a nine-hole pitch n' putt course at **Prospect Reef Resort**, just west of Road Town. Check in at the activities desk. Small fee for non-guests.

Avid golfers can take an early ferry (or flight) to St. Thomas, play 18 holes at **Mahogany Run** golf course, and ferry back.

Tennis

Tortola's tennis options revolve around the island's hotels. Some have pro shops and a tennis professional on staff and others have courts but no pro. All the hotels below allow non-guests to play for a fee of about $15 per hour.

Tip: Try to avoid playing in the midday sun. Make reservations.

Long Bay Beach Resort, ☎ (284) 495-4252. Three courts and professional management. Racket rentals.

Prospect Reef Resort, ☎ (284) 494-3311. Several hard-surface courts that can be lit for night play. Pro.

Frenchman's Cay, ☎ (284) 495-4844. An artificial grass court that stands beside the channel. Can be lit for night play. No pro.

Mooring's Mariner Inn, ☎ (284) 494-3444. One all-weather court. No pro. Not always in A-1 shape.

Lambert Beach Resort, ☎ (284) 495-2877. One court that can be lit. No pro. The resort is accessed via a difficult road to drive at night.

Horseback Riding

Shadow's Stables, Ridge Road, ☎ (284) 494-2262. Rides begin at the stable and follow the winding and dramatic Ridge Road (across the mountain chain) to Sage Mountain National Park, located at Tortola's highest point. Other rides follow Ridge Road to Cane Garden Bay. Rides cost about $50 per hour and half that for kids.

Cycling

Last Stop Sports, Nanny Cay, ☎ (284) 494-0564. Rents mountain bikes for both adults and children. They deliver to your hotel.

Spectator Sports

Cricket is extremely popular. International matches are often televised here. The BVI has a cricket league and games are played on weekends from February-June. Matches are played at the **A.O. Shirley Recreation Grounds**, next to the Botanic Gar-

Tortola

dens, Road Town. Check at the Tourist kiosk at the
Road Town Ferry Dock to see if a match is scheduled
during your stay.

Hiking

Sage Mountain National Park

 Sage Mountain, at 1,780 feet, is the highest
point in the BVI. The National Park, which
covers 92 acres, is criss-crossed with trails
– none of them difficult to hike. The trails
are marked and signs will alert you to the
different varieties of plants growing here. While it
doesn't get enough rain to actually be a rainforest,
parts of the park look just like one. Vine-covered
trees, mosses, orchids and philodendrons are prominent. **Slippery Path** (only when wet) leads from the
parking lot to a grove of prehistoric ferns that have
existed since the Coal Age, 200 million years ago.
They stand 20 feet high and have delicate green
fronds. Mahogany and kapok trees are also in the
park. There are picnic tables and great views of Jost
Van Dyke.

Getting Here: From West End, take Zion Hill
Road (across the island) to North Coast Road to
Ridge Road. Follow the signs to Sage Mountain
Road. From Road Town, take Great Mountain Road
to Ridge Road. Look for road signs to the villages of
Doty and Chalwell.

Brewer's Bay Beach & Windmill Ruin

Brewer's is a magnificent beach with a small campground. There is fine snorkeling here. From the
beach there is a steep trail leading to the ruins of an
18th-century plantation and the remnants of an old
windmill that was used to crush the sugar cane for

molasses and rum. This area, now a national park, is called **Mt. Healthy**.

Getting Here: Take Ridge Road to Brewer's Bay Road East.

Sightseeing

Exploring Road Town

Road Town is a small West Indian town with only a few streets and areas of interest to visitors. The two most important streets are Sir Francis Drake Highway (Waterfront Drive) and Main Street. Both follow the curve of the channel and are lined by buildings painted in pastel shades with contrasting shutters. They have steep corrugated roofs and intricate fretwork (gingerbread trim). Virtually 90% of the population lives in or near Road Town, but the residential areas are in the hills behind the commercial center.

The busiest section of Waterfront Drive is near the Ferry Dock and the Customs House. With ferries the lifeline of these islands, this area is always bustling. Pusser's Pub is directly across the street and there are many other restaurants as you follow Waterfront Drive, going east or west.

There is a small parking lot here.

There is no "don't miss" sight in Road Town, but you'll enjoy a stroll through it so we'll point out a few historic buildings. Main Street, the second street from the harbor, is narrow and winding. It has several historic buildings and cafés and shops. Look for **Government House**, west of the ferry dock (near Cedar Road), which commands an imposing position overlooking the harbor. It was the official residence of the Governor, who was appointed by the British. Built in 1926, the building is visible from the harbor

Road Town

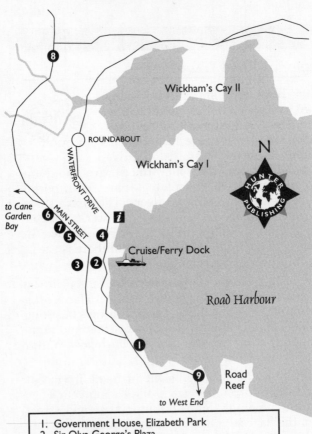

1. Government House, Elizabeth Park
2. Sir Olva George's Plaza
3. Post Office
4. Virgin Island Folk Museum
5. St. George's Anglican Church
6. Methodist Church
7. Old HM Prison
8. J.R. O'Neil Botanical Gardens
9. Fort Burt

NOT TO SCALE   © 2005 HUNTER PUBLISHING, INC and marked by Union Jacks on a flagpole. Recently renovated, it now houses a small museum. The park here is **Elizabeth Park**.

The small plaza that opens on both Waterfront Drive and Main Street is **Sir Olva Georges' Plaza**, a charming resting spot that was once the town's market.

On Main Street, behind the plaza stands the post office that is housed in the 19th-century **Commissioner's Office and Court House**. BVI stamps are lovely and many people collect them. Only the ground floor has the original stone walls and brick arches.

The **Virgin Island Folk Museum**, in a yellow traditional building, has artifacts from the island's plantation and slavery eras and pieces from the wreck of RMS *Rhone*. This museum has been undergoing renovation for as long as we can remember.

Three other historic buildings are a short distance away. Two are churches. **St. George's Anglican Church** has Georgian features. The first Anglican priest arrived here in 1746. The core of the church was rebuilt after an 1819 hurricane. A cool resting place, the church houses the 1834 Emancipation Proclamation. The **Methodist Church** was built shortly after Methodists came to Tortola in 1789. The original church also fell victim to a hurricane in 1924. This new building is marked by a stone walkway inscribed with the names of prominent members of the church.

Between the two churches is the **Old HM Prison** that housed prisoners till a new facility was built near Lambert Bay. Constructed in the 18th century, the building was designed and altered to suit the needs of the prison officials.

Tortola

If you continue to follow Main Street for approximately 20 minutes, you'll come to the **J.R. O'Neal Botanic Gardens**. A lovely oasis, run by the National Parks Trust, it opened in 1987. Covering just under three acres, the park showcases some of the great variety of Caribbean flowers and herbs. Most interesting is the mini-forest, with exotic plants shaded by huge saman trees. Nearby, the Fern House has a large collection of West Indies ferns from Sage Mountain. There is a Christmas Garden and a fascinating medicinal plant section.

The gardens are maintained by local volunteers. The plants are arranged according to habitat in sections reached by landscaped paths radiating from a three-tiered fountain. The orchid house and a small rainforest are reached by crossing a charming lily pond. Other paths lead to a cactus garden and a palm grove. On Main Street (a 15-minute walk from the post office). Open Mon-Sat 9 am-4:30 pm.

Return to Waterfront Drive, cross the thoroughfare, and you'll find yourself on **Wickham's Cay I**, a complex that includes a Craft Fair, government buildings, shopping centers, restaurants and a marina.

Islandwide Sights

Callwood Rum Distillery

Located in the woods off North Shore Road in Cane Garden Bay (ask anyone to point the way), Callwood's is one of just a handful of functioning distilleries left in the BVI. Mr. Callwood, a rather grumpy type, charges $3 for a fifth. It's potent stuff.

North Shore Shell Museum

In Carrot Bay, this informal exhibit shows a variety of shells, unusually shaped driftwood, fish traps and traditional wooden boats. Fun for kids. North Shore Road.

Josiah's Bay Plantation

Once part of a 19th-century sugar plantation, Josiah's Bay plantation was converted into a rum distillery during the American Prohibition era. The grounds have a rum still, vats and other relics. Part of the building has been restored and houses "A Secret Garden Restaurant" and an art gallery. Ridge Road to Josiah's Bay Road.

St. Philips Church, Kingstown

The walls of St. Philip's Church are virtually all that remain of the free African settlement at Kingstown. When slavery was abolished in 1807, Africans on British ships were liberated. Some were brought to Tortola. The British government purchased land and distributed it in 1831. One year later over a hundred cottages had been built and over 300 people lived here. St. Philip's was an Anglican church and a school. Follow Water Front Drive east of Road Town to Kingstown.

Forts

Many Caribbean islands have remains of forts built at the entrances to harbors by the Dutch to ward off French or by the British to ward off Spanish pirates. Tortola is no exception. **Fort Recovery** is a well-preserved tower built by Tortola's earliest Dutch settlers. It's at Fort Recovery Villas, West End. **Fort Burt** is perched at the entrance to Road Harbour. A hotel has been built on its foundations but cannons and a well-preserved stone magazine is on the grounds. Look for Fort Burt Hotel up a narrow hill just west of Road Town.

Tortola

Flightseeing

If you'd like to see this beautiful area from the air, consider a flight with **Fly BVI**. Trips last 45 minutes and cruise at 1,000 feet, offering astonishing views and photo ops. They also run an Anegada day-trip that includes a lobster lunch. ☎ (284) 495-1247, www.fly-bvi.com.

Island Helicopters also offers sightseeing tours and an Anegada trip. ☎ (284) 499-2663, www.helicoptersbvi.com.

The Best Shops

Tortola has many shops that you'll enjoy browsing in. They are small and locally owned. No Gap or Eddie Bauer here. Main Street is Road Town's shopping street, but there are many good shops at the three mini-malls on Wickham's Cay I, at Soper's Hole Marina, West End and scattered elsewhere. Start at the post office and stop into those that catch your eye.

> **Tip:** If you are a serious shopper and want to buy fine china, crystal or jewelry, take the ferry to St. Thomas for the day.

Hours

Stores in Road Town are generally open Monday-Saturday, 9-5. Those at Soper's Hole sometimes stay open till 7 pm.

Tips

Credit cards (Visa and MC) are accepted in virtually every store. American Express in fewer. It's a good idea to have some traveler's checks or cash for the few that are holdouts.

Shops here open for one season and close when it ends, except for the handful that remain year after year. Usually, a similar shop occupies the space for the next season so don't be put off if you can't find the shop we've listed. Stroll into everything that looks interesting.

Main Street

Pusser's Company Store is a wood-paneled shop that sells its own famous BVI rums in a variety of souvenir bottles, plus nautical antiques and memorabilia and Pusser-designed shorts, mugs, T-shirts and canvas bags.

Latitude 18 sells casual clothing and accessories for men, women and children. Scarves, T-shirts, bathing suits and pareos, as well as Sunny Caribbean herbs and jams. Also in Soper's Hole.

Sunny Caribbee Herb & Spice Co. is Tortola's most attractive and best-smelling shop. It sells its own herbs, spices, teas, coffees, sauces and vinegar, as well as soaps and lotions. Adjoining the herb store, the **Sunny Caribbee Art Gallery** sells colorful paintings and prints, ceramics and collages with island themes.

Samarkand features handcrafted silver and gold jewelry by a husband-and-wife artisan team. Many items have Caribbean themes.

Al Baraza carries clothes, sculptures, musical instruments and books from Africa.

Little Denmark is not an attractive store, but it has a walk-in humidor for cigars – many from Cuba.

Absolutely Fabulous sells all-natural organic bath and beauty products, scented candles and fragrances.

Tortola

You can bargain at the Crafts Market, but elsewhere all shops hold to a fixed-price policy.

Serendipity/Domino is a terrific bookstore with bestsellers, books about the Caribbean and a variety of nonfiction. The Domino part sells lovely gift items.

Caribbean Fine Arts Tropical Gallery features a large selection of BVI and regional paintings, pottery and primitives.

Wickham's Cay I

Crafts Alive Market & House of Crafts at the entrance to the Cay sells locally made goods in straw, ceramic, wood, hand-painted T-shirts and island sauces and jellies.

Columbian Emeralds, a company that has shops on virtually every Caribbean Island, sells emerald jewelry primarily but also diamonds and colorful gemstones. It's the most upscale store in town.

Sea Urchin, at Mill Mall, is shaped like a lighthouse. It sells resort wear, casual sportswear, sunglasses, swimsuits, sandals, postcards and more. Other Sea Urchin shops are on Waterfront Drive (near Pusser's) and in Soper's Hole.

Kidd's Korner, in the Cutlass building, sells childrens' clothing with colorful island themes.

Ample Hamper is a gourmet deli with a wide selection of wines and imported English products. Also in Soper's Hole and Hodge's Creek Marina.

Near Road Town

Shirt Shack, in a West Indian house, features casual cottons and resort wear. On Chalwell Street, a small street that connects Main Street to Waterfront Drive.

Kadir's House of Exquisite Pieces, also on Chalwell Street, sells fine silver and gold jewelry, with many one-of-a-kind pieces.

HIHO, in J.R. O'Neal Plaza, sells surf apparel, sandals, and other surf supplies, including boards.

Voila, in Road Reef Plaza (near Prospect Reef Resort, west of town), sells unique home accessories. Colorful ceramics and glassware, ethic items inspired by African artisans, unusual picture frames and hand-made journals.

Soper's Hole Marina

On Frenchman's Cay at Tortola's West End, the Soper's Hole Wharf and Marina is a popular dining and shopping venue.

Pusser's Landing & Co. Store sells its brands of rum, as well as hats, T-shirts and canvas bags.

Sea Urchin has beachwear, hats and shoes, sunglasses and tropical fashions.

BVI Apparel also has cotton T-shirts, embroidered polos and gift items.

Latitude 18 sells casual clothing and accessories for the whole family.

Pat's Pottery offers locally designed and produced artwork and pottery.

Ample Hamper sells gourmet groceries, provisions and wines.

Zenaida has sarongs, clothing and accessories printed in their own studio.

Islandwide

Arawak, at Nanny Cay Resort (West) and Hodge's Creek Marina (East), features Indian batik fashions designed in the BVI.

Josiah's Bay Plantation, in Josiah's Bay, has a lovely art gallery and furniture shop.

Fluke's Gift Shop and Gallery, at Trellis Bay (Beef Island), sells prints and maps.

Tortola

Aragorn's Studios, also at Trellis Bay, has hand-painted T-shirts, baskets, sculptures, Carib Indian crafts and clothing.

Bamboushay is a fine arts center that has pottery and a kiln so you can see items being made. Every item is individually hand-crafted on-site. Nanny Cay Marina.

Olivia's Gift Shop, Myett's Garden, Cane Garden Bay, has some very interesting gift items, books on reggae and the BVI, CDs of island musicians, tropical fashions and accessories.

Best Places to Stay

There is no hotel strip on Tortola. An eclectic group, hotels lie on stunning North Shore beaches, on hillsides overlooking Road Town harbor, alongside marinas and in ancient forts and sugar cane plantations.

Without exception, the hotels are small (only two have over 40 rooms), informal and rustic. They accurately mirror Tortola's slow-paced, rural ambience. No luxury here, but lots of comfort, friendly faces and complete serenity. If you really mean to get away from the outside world, you can do so easily here. TV sets are rare, as is air conditioning. Kitchenettes are commonplace and many hotels have commissaries and laundromats. Resort hotels have good restaurants and pools. They offer a wide range of water-related sports. Those without spacious grounds whisk you to private beach clubs on islands in the channel.

Some hotels accommodate guests in villas, as well as in rooms and suites. These on-property villas commonly have two bedrooms, which gives guests, especially families with children, more living space, a measure of privacy and the option of preparing some meals "at home." Villas have full resort amenities.

There are also many villas and houses for rent that are individually owned and not part of a hotel complex. Many are represented by Stateside agencies. See page 79 for details.

Guesthouses are another option to consider on Tortola, where lodgings are always tight in season.

Because there are so few hotel rooms, they are at a premium during the winter season (December 15-April 15). Naturally, rates are highest during this time. You should make arrangements as much as a year in advance. If you plan to visit at other times of the year, rates fall dramatically, in some cases by as much as 30%. Package tours (hotel plus boat or hotel plus air), honeymoon or scuba are available.

Tortola

The Alive Scale

To give you a ballpark figure to budget with, we have devised the scale below. It is based on the price of a double room in high season.

Expensive . . . . over $250
Moderate . . . . $150-$250
Inexpensive . . . . under $150

Money Matters: Hotels accept major credit cards. Some smaller spots (cottages, guesthouses) prefer a check as down payment on your reservation. Find out which credit cards are accepted when making your reservation. Hotels add a 7% government tax to your rate as well as a 10% service charge daily. If air conditioning or a TV set is important to you, specify that when booking.

Long Bay Beach Resort Villas

Box 433, Road Town
Tortola, BVI
☎ (284) 495-4252
www.longbay.com
Moderate-Expensive

Secluded on a 52-acre hillside and along a one-mile
North Shore beach (the island's loveliest), Long Bay
Beach Resort does not even mark its entrance with a
sign. With 80 guest rooms, 10 suites and 26 villas, it
is Tortola's largest hotel. Because the grounds are so
spacious, the hotel can cater to those who want privacy and those who enjoy activity, be they honey-
mooners, couples, families or singles.

Hillside guestrooms are set about 100 yards from
the beach in small multiple-story units. The deluxe
versions are a bit closer to the beach with some located around the Pelican Pool and sun deck. Both
have light tropical woods, designer fabrics and balconies or decks facing the sea. Jacuzzi suites are also
on the hillside. Private and peaceful, they have
king-sized beds, separate sitting areas and whirlpool tubs in the bedroom. Here, too, a balcony or
deck overlooks the grounds and ocean. Beachfront
rooms are similar to those on the hillside but are
larger to accommodate families.

Personal favorites are the dozen gray beachfront ca-
banas that stand on stilts behind the beach. The oldest accommodations here, they are cleverly tucked
behind seagrape trees, hibiscus and frangipani
bushes. All guestrooms are air-conditioned, have cable TVs, coffee makers, refrigerators and safes.

The two- and three-bedroom villas have large, comfortable living rooms, with cable TVs, VCRs and full
kitchens. The large deck has room for outside seating and a gas grill.

Long Bay management acts as a rental agent for villas located near the resort. Guests have full hotel privileges.

A restored sugar mill at the Beach Pool serves as a bar and socializing place as well as a breakfast and lunch nook. Informal dinners and special buffets are served here as well. There's music several nights a week too. The Garden Restaurant in the main building is a gourmet dining room. It serves continental food and is open only for dinner. Reservations are a must and casual chic attire (but no jackets) is required.

With two swimming pools and a mile-long beach, Long Bay is perfect for swimming, snorkeling and body surfing. There are two artificial grass tennis courts, which can be lit for night play and a single hard court near the Beach Café. The latest addition to Long Bay is the Spa and Fitness Center, in an arcade adjacent to the main building. The spa offers a variety of beauty and wellness treatments and the fitness center has treadmills, bicycles, stairmasters and weight training equipment. Reservations for the spa through Ultra Resorts, ☎ (914) 833-3300.

The Sugar Mill Hotel
Box 425, Road Town
Tortola, BVI
☎ (284) 495-4355
www.sugarmillhotel.com
Closed August & September
Expensive

Jinx and Jeff Morgan, two savvy California-based food critics and cookbook authors, took a faded small hotel and turned it into a sophisticated hideaway with a gourmet restaurant. Built over 300 years ago as a sugar mill plantation, the main building was constructed from stone and brick ballast. Parts of

A delightful North Shore hideaway on Little Apple Bay.

these historic walls now house the resort's dining room and bar/sitting alcove.

On a shallow hillside just off North Shore Road, the hotel's 24 redwood and stucco units peek out from behind tropical palms and flowering bushes. The Plantation House is a recent addition. It houses two two-bedroom suites that have king-sized beds and comfortable sitting areas. The suites, cottages and studios are attractively furnished and air-conditioned. Each has a small library, kitchen facilities, comfortable beds and seating areas, with some colorful local art. Some have a queen-size sofa bed for kids to sleep on.

Breakfast has a large help-yourself coffee urn, freshly baked muffins and coconut bread along with homemade jam. Lunch served at Islands, a sand bar restaurant, consists of burgers, sandwiches and salads made with greens grown at the hotel. Informal dinners are also served here in season.

You must reserve for dinner in the Sugar Mill Restaurant. It usually has four courses and is prix fixe but you can order à la carte as well. Selections vary each night. (See page 82 for details).

There is a raised circular pool, sun deck and lounge chairs, an honor bar and ping pong. A small beach is across the road.

Lambert Beach Resort & Villas
Box 534, East End
Tortola, BVI
☎ (284) 495-2877
www.lambertbeachresort.com
Moderate-Expensive

Working too hard? Hiding out from the mob? Want a beach to call your own? If you've answered yes to any or all of the above, you should consider Lambert Beach Resort, the newest resort on Tortola. Lambert

Bay is on the island's northeastern coast and really off the beaten track. Look for the sign to Lambert Bay from Ridge Road. Soon you'll see the red-pitched rooftops far below you. Down below you'll find 36 rooms in eight cottages. There are also two suites. The cottages are linked by beautifully landscaped walkways and are strung behind the seagrape trees that line the beach. Rooms are large, painted white with brown beamed ceilings and feature colorful rugs and drapes. Each has a private patio.

The beach is long and lovely with rolling waves just right for the sea kayaks, boogie boarding, and snorkeling. Gear rental, including beach volleyballs, is available at the watersports kiosk. There is a good-size pool with a sundeck and a swim-up bar. They have a snack bar at poolside as well. There is one tennis court.

Guests gather for dinner at Turtles, the beachfront eatery, where the menu is Italian and includes pizza. After dinner, they head to the open-air clubhouse, which has comfortable sitting areas, stone walls and board games. There's a communal TV and a used-book library.

Lambert Beach Resort is a casual, secluded hideaway about 20 minutes by car from Road Town.

> **NOTE:** Lambert Beach Resort manages two- and three-bedroom villas on the same bay set back farther from the beach. Villa guests can use all the resort amenities.

Prospect Reef Resort

Box 104, Road Town
Tortola, BVI
☎ (284) 494-3311
www.prospectreef.com
Closed August and September
Moderate

With 137 rooms, this is the second-largest resort on Tortola. Set on Slaney Point, its 44 acres front Sir

Drake Channel, which is terrific for
...ts. However, because the resort does not
...tural sand beach (just a man-made one) it
...ests to private beach areas on Peter Island
... Van Dyke. Each has watersports gear. The
...ant, Callaloo on the Beach, is a great perk.

...ct Reef has recently been purchased by new
owners who have a done a terrific job of refurbishing
the accommodations and upgrading the facilities.
Winding paths criss-cross the spacious grounds,
which are beautifully landscaped. As you enter the
property, you'll see the resort's freshwater pool, as
well as a small shopping arcade. The two restaurants are here as well.

Accommodations are scattered through the property. They vary from rather simple studios (second
floor, ceiling fans) to attractive suites and villas that
have tile floors, contemporary furnishings with island touches and air-conditioning. All rooms have
satellite TVs, clock radios, direct dial phones, personal safes and mini-refrigerators.

The beach res-
taurants serve
till 9:30 pm so
you can enjoy
a leisurely
dinner before
returning to
the Reef.

There is a sea pool on property, a spa and fitness
center (the spa is open to the public), a pitch n' putt
golf course and several tennis courts. Prospect Reef
has a highly regarded marina.

Scuttlebutt, an open-air pub, serves Caribbean specialties and sandwiches/salads from 11 am daily,
while Callaloo at the Reef serves dinner and an
eclectic mix of foods.

Fort Recovery Beach Resort
Box 239, Road Town
Tortola, BVI
☎ (284) 495-4467
www.fortrecovery.com
Moderate-Expensive

An unusual stop, Fort Recovery sits on a secluded
beach on Drake's Channel and the view from its vil-

las includes St. John and the passing sailboats. Sea-side villas are the sole accommodations at this hideaway. Built around an original 17th-century Dutch fort, they are accented with oleander, hibiscus and bougainvillea. Villas have one to four bedrooms. Management calls the four-bedroom villa, a "house." The Penthouse villa has beamed cathedral ceilings and designer furnishings. All the villas are spacious and tastefully furnished. They have fully equipped kitchens, living rooms with comfortable sofas, TV sets and air conditioners. All have private balconies or patios. Maid service and continental breakfast are included.

There is a pool, but most guests head to the private beach, which is equipped with a water trampoline.

Special features include gourmet dinners, prepared in the restaurant and served course-by-course in your villa or on the candlelit deck. Yoga classes and massages are also available. The staff is very friendly and guests are drawn from all parts of the US.

Fort Burt Hotel
Box 3380, Road Town
Tortola, BVI
☎ (284) 494-2587
www.bviguide.com/fortburt
Moderate-Expensive

On a knoll just west of Road Town, this circular hotel and adjacent restaurant incorporating the ruins of an ancient Dutch fort (built in 1666) are high above the channel. The Dutch soldiers kept a watchful eye for approaching enemy vessels, but you can relax on your private balcony and watch the graceful sailing ships and plodding ferries pass by. The dozen rooms are decorated in muted tones with white wicker, tile floors and kitchenettes. The six suites are newer. Two deluxe suites have their own pools.

The hotel was for a time managed by Pusser's Company, but has returned to private hands.

The Fort Burt Restaurant has a striking peaked roof and both an indoor dining room and a verandah. It serves Caribbean and Continental cuisine.

The small marina on the channel below houses another restaurant, The Pub, which is a popular watering hole. It serves British specialties.

The long, narrow roadway leading up to the hotel can be tough at night, but you'll get used to it. An unusual stop but a very tasteful one.

Frenchman's Cay Hotel
Box 1054, West End
Tortola, BVI
☎ (284) 495-4844
www.frenchmans.cay
Expensive

Set on its own 12-acre island just one mile from the West End ferry dock and adjacent to Soper's Wharf's shops, Frenchman's Cay can be reached by car over a very narrow bridge.

Frenchman's Cay has a library with over 700 volumes for guest use.

There are nine freestanding villas and these are strung along a hillside overlooking the public facilities on the shore below. There are one- and two-bedroom villas. Each can sleep an additional two people on a queen-size sleeping sofa in the sitting area. Furnishings are contemporary, using bold prints, florals and rattan so popular here. All villas have kitchens and daily maid service. They do not have air conditioning or TV sets. There is a communal TV in the Clubhouse.

There is a freshwater pool and one tennis court. You can snorkel over a shallow reef offshore. The area is dry; prominent in the landscaping are rock gardens and cactus shrubs.

An attractive building with an unusual peaked roof houses The Clubhouse Restaurant. Breakfast, lunch and dinner are served every day. The chef features grilled fish and barbecued meats. From the bar, St. John, USVI, looks close enough to swim to.

Sebastian's On the Beach & Seaside Villas
Box 441, Road Town
Tortola, BVI
☎ (284) 495-4212
www.sebastiansbvi.com
Moderate/Expensive

Sebastian's On the Beach is like a pair of old shoes – not great looking but very comfortable and inviting. On Little Apple Bay, at the foot of the mountain range that forms the island's spine, it has a winning beachfront location. One of the oldest hotels here, the original building was opened over 30 years ago. It now houses simply furnished rooms with twin beds or basic suites with two queen-sized beds, mini-refrigerators and ceiling fans. A few of these rooms are air-conditioned.

In sharp contrast to the accommodations above, Sebastian's has added a villa that contains luxurious suites. Two bedrooms plus a sleeping sofa in the living room make them comfortable for eight. All the units are air-conditioned, have TVs and VCRs and there is a film library. Bathrooms are large, with marble floors and showers. Each unit has a balcony facing the bay. Two of the suites have teak whirlpool baths in the oversized bathrooms.

Sebastian's restaurant is set on the beach. It features West Indian food and is best known for its exotic rum drinks. Music plays at dinner several nights a week. No pool here, but the beach shack has surfboards, windsurf boards, Sunfish and beach tennis gear. Villa guests can use all the equipment without charge.

Sebastian's is so informal that dressing for dinner means putting on shorts and a T-shirt.

By the way, body surfers from the US and other Caribbean isles flock to Little Apple Bay during the winter when the waves are right for serious body-surfing. Not fancy, but fun.

Ole Works Inn

Box 560, Cane Garden Bay
Tortola, BVI
☎ (284) 495-4837
www.bviguide.com/ole.html
Inexpensive

A charming 18-room hostelry built on a 320-year-old restored sugar factory, Ole Works Inn is owned by singer Quito Rhymer and is directly across the road from his restaurant. (See *Best Places to Stay*, page 88). There are several views from the rooms; those facing Cane Garden Bay are the most expensive. Rooms are small and simply furnished with double beds, air conditioners, refrigerators and clock radios. The honeymoon tower and junior suite are larger and have TVs and kitchenettes. The hotel is well-maintained.

Cane Garden Bay Beach Hotel

Box 570, Cane Garden Bay
Tortola, BVI
☎ (284) 495-4639
www.bviguide.com/rhymers.html
Inexpensive

Cane Garden Bay Beach is the most developed area on Tortola's northern shore. The long beach is dotted with seagrapes and coconut palms, with private homes, churches and schools and the island's best West Indian restaurants.

Cane Garden Beach Hotel is part of a locally owned hotel/restaurant complex and is the liveliest spot on the beach. The hotel's 24 rooms are modest in size and simply furnished, but they do have air conditioners and TVs, twin or queen-sized beds, dressing tables, rocking chairs, and kitchenettes. The adjacent beachfront restaurant serves all three meals and has a steel band, guitar or calypso singer to liven up dinner. Charter boats anchor offshore and crew members quaff beer and swap tales at this restaurant.

An inexpensive option on a fine beach.

The beach shack rents windsurf boards, Hobie Cats, dinghies, lounges and paddleboats. There's a grocery and laundromat too.

Myette's Garden Inn
Box 556, Cane Garden Bay
Tortola, BVI
☎ (284) 495-9649
www.myettent.com
Inexpensive

This tiny inn has only three rooms – two that face the gardens and one that faces the beach. They are all air-conditioned with king-size beds and tile floors. The rooms are large enough to have a sitting area, with loveseats, wicker chairs and tables in light-colored woods and colorful print fabrics. Bathrooms are small. There is a fridge, wet bar and coffee maker, but no cooking facilities. Since the property is in the heart of the most developed beach area on the island, you can eat at a score of nearby spots, rent watersports gear and small boats and have an enjoyable nightlife, all within five minutes.

Moorings-Mariner Inn
Box 139, Wickham's Cay II, Road Town
Tortola, BVI
☎ (284) 494-2333
Moderate

The Moorings, just east of Road Town, is the largest marina in the BVI, with dockage for 90 boats. The adjacent Mariners Inn is overshadowed by the activity dockside, but is actually a comfortable hotel with a surprising range of facilities. Most people use it as a jumping-off point for chartering or a last stop before heading home.

Tortola

Moorings also manages the Treasure Isle Hotel (below) across Waterfront Drive. Guests move between facilities.

The 40 pink bi-level units look much like a Stateside motel, with terraces overlooking the marina. They have kitchenettes and ceiling fans. There are two large suites for families.

There is a good-sized swimming pool by the dock, tennis court and a small restaurant where the chit-chat revolves around buying a yacht, renting one or planning your life so you can do one of the above. On the same cove, a supermarket, liquor store and dive shop co-exist with yacht repair shops and the like.

Treasure Isle Hotel
Box 68, Road Town
Tortola, BVI
☎ (284) 494-2501
www.treasureislehotel.net
Moderate

Action-oriented and drawing a friendly crowd of return visitors, Treasure Isle was the first real resort on Tortola. The hotel consists of a series of faded yellow buildings set into the hillside at varying levels, overlooking Road Town harbor and islands in the channel. You can drive most of the way up the hill to access units. The lowest level houses the reception desk, activities center, pool, shops and the Lime n' Mango Restaurant. Individual rooms are farther uphill. The hotel's other facilities are located nearby.

Treasure Isle is a friendly spot to meet people, especially if you are a first-time visitor.

Management of Treasure Isle has been taken over by The Moorings-Mariner Inn (directly across the road), so the hotel is now part of the Moorings complex. There is an excellent dive center and, of course, the yacht rental agency. A five-minute walk will bring you to the tennis courts.

The Lime n' Mango Restaurant serves both Caribbean specialties and Mexican ones at dinner each night, except Saturday when they have a barbecue.

Since there is no beach, the hotels operate a launch service to Cooper Island, where you can swim, snorkel and eat.

Village Cay Resort & Marina
Box 145, Road Town
Tortola, BVI
☎ (284) 494-2771
www.villagecay.com
Moderate

On Wickham's Cay I, facing the marina in the heart of Road Town, this small stop with 19 rooms is popular with yachties. Not all the rooms are the same – some have cathedral ceilings, some face the harbor and some are quite small. They are decorated in pastel prints and natural rattan, are air-conditioned and have cable TVs. The hotel has no lobby or entertainment areas, but it does have a popular restaurant and spa facilities. The Village Cay Dockside Restaurant is most crowded at lunch. It serves fresh fish, lobster and steaks.

Nanny Cay Resort & Marina
Box 281, Road Town
Tortola, BVI
☎ (234) 494-2512
www.nannycay.com
Moderate

Nanny Cay, an islet midway between Road Town and West End, is a small area built around a vibrant marina. It has shops, restaurants and a small hotel. Many of the guests at this 40-room property are involved with the marina. Rooms in the pink stucco, bi-level building have air conditioning, TVs, VCRs and kitchenettes. There is a small beach and sports equipment is available for rent. There are two pools. One is part of Peg Leg Landing, one of our listed restaurants (see page 95). This is a bustling area much like Village Cay and not as secluded as a North Shore choice.

Maria's Hotel By The Sea

Box 206, Road Town
Tortola, BVI
☎ (284) 494-2595
www.mariabythesea.com
Moderate

Prices seem high for what you get here.

Under the same management as the Hotel Castle Maria (below), this hotel is right in Road Town. The 38 units abut the harbor and are a two-minute walk to Road Town shops, restaurants and the ferry dock. They are small and furnished in tropical style with bright fabrics and wicker and have kitchenettes or wet bars, TV sets and are air-conditioned. Individual balconies face the channel or a palm-filled courtyard. There is a small pool and a public restaurant on the premises.

Hotel Castle Maria

Box 206, Road Town
Tortola, BVI
☎ (284) 494-2553
www.islandsonline.com/hotelcastlemaria
Inexpensive

A good choice for active vacationers who don't spend much time in their rooms and aren't concerned about creature comforts. The three-story building curves along the side of a hill at the western edge of Road Town (look for the sign). The large rooms, off a long hall with an interesting mural, have air conditioners or fans, kitchenettes, refrigerators and some are full efficiency apartments. There is a small pool and sun deck. The second-floor lobby and bar has a TV and management is very helpful. The hotel restaurant, Fusions, offers a view of Road Harbour and fusion cuisine, including pastas and seafood. It serves dinner from 7 pm.

Villa Rentals

Many visitors to the BVI opt to stay at a villa, cottage or apartment that is not part of a hotel complex. The villas are individually owned and furnished, ranging from incredibly deluxe to delightfully rustic. Maid service, cable TVs, VCRs, washer/dryers and a host of other amenities may or may not be included. There are scores of such villas and the best way to find them is to contact a management firm that represents several.

Areana Villas, Box 263, Road Town, represents the top-of-the-line villas with private pools, Jacuzzis and stunning views. ☎ (284) 494-5864, www. areanavillas.com.

McLaughlin Anderson Luxury Villas, 1000 Blackbeard's Hill, Suite 3, St. Thomas, VI 00802, represents family hideaways, apartments and romantic retreats. ☎ (800) 537-6246, www.mclaughlinanderson. com.

Heritage Villas, Box 2019, Carrot Bay, represents the villa community on a hillside overlooking Carrot Bay. There are one- and two-bedroom villas with great views. ☎ (284) 494-5842, www.heritagevillasbvi. com.

British Virgin Islands Villas, Box 8309, Cruz Bay, St. John's USVI, represents lower-priced villa options. ☎ (284) 494-2442, www.britishvirginvillas. com.

My Private Paradise, 1305 4th Street SW, Washington, DC 20024, represents a broad range of villas. ☎ (800) 862-7863, www.myprivateparadise.com.

Tortola

Apartments & Cottages

Cane Garden Bay Cottages. Reasonably priced cottages nestled among coconut palms. Each cottage sleeps four. Full maid service, full kitchens or kitchenettes, screened porch for eating or relaxing. A one-minute walk to the beach. ☎ (284) 495-3100, www.purplepineapple. com/cgbcottages.html.

Coconut Point Vacation Apartments. An attractive pastel West Indian house on Apple Bay houses four rental apartments. Some are two-bedroom and others are studios. Each has different amenities. Set in a garden setting with bananas and tropical fruit trees. ☎ (284) 495-4892, www.go-bvi.com/coconut-point.

Best Places to Dine

 Tortola is laid-back and informal and so are most of its eateries. You will be surprised at the number and variety of dining options here. Restaurants – some sophisticated and gourmet, others casual and intimate – are scattered throughout the island. In cheerfully painted typical West Indian houses, at seaside and marinas, in Road Town's historic buildings or in the ruins of old sugar mills, restaurants here boast eclectic menus with foods garnered from all parts of the globe. Many of the hotels have good restaurants as well.

Because most foodstuffs are imported, prices are higher than you might expect. Seafood dishes are often the least expensive items on the menu because there is an abundance of freshly caught fish and shellfish. The majority of Tortola's restaurants are moderately priced and informal. They are fun to eat in and, while the goods served may be less imaginative than dishes served in the gourmet stops, they are well prepared and often delicious. These include the island's West Indian eateries – short on décor but long on local fish, Johnny cakes (fried bread), conch fritters and goat curry. You should definitely put aside one evening and head to Carrot Bay and Cane Garden Bay where the best West Indian places are located. It's a great way to meet local people too.

Dining Tips

Tortola

As you might expect, dress in the gourmet restaurants is more formal (long pants, collared shirts, no ties), but there are many spots where you can dine in shorts and T-shirts.

Tortola is an early-to-rise island, as is most of the Caribbean. Dinner starts and ends early. Restaurants typically serve from 6:30 to 10 pm, with 7:30-8:30 being prime time.

Restaurants are quite small so it makes sense to reserve for dinner. In some restaurants it is imperative, since the chef cooks to the house. In high season, reserve in advance at the gourmet eateries.

Virtually all restaurants take MasterCard and Visa, and some also take American Express. A few West Indian places still do not take credit cards.

There are fine dining options in many of the previously mentioned hotels – the **Garden Restaurant** at Long Bay Beach Hotel and **Callaloo on the Reef** at Prospect Reef Hotel come to mind. We have not included hotel restaurants in this section, however, except for Restaurant, which is exceptional. Exploring restaurants in different parts of the island and sampling a variety of foods is one of the most enjoyable aspects of being on Tortola.

To that end we have selected restaurants in Road Town, on the island's North Shore and at East and West End. Driving distances are not great so, no matter where you are staying, you are an easy drive away.

The Alive Scale

To give you some idea of how much dinner will cost, we have devised the Alive Scale. It is based on a three-course dinner plus coffee (per person, no alcoholic beverages).

Expensive . . . . over $45
Moderate . . . . $30-$45
Inexpensive . . . . under $30

Exceptional Dining

The Sugar Mill
Sugar Mill Hotel
Apple Bay (North Shore)
☎ (284) 495-4355
Expensive
Dinner only 7-9 pm

Rarely is the food in a hotel's restaurant worth driving cross-island for, but the Sugar Mill Hotel Restaurant is definitely worth the trip. The setting – in a 300-year-old sugar mill – is romantic, and flickering candles heighten the effect. Dinner consists of four courses, all planned and coordinated by owners Jinx and Jeff Morgan, who are well-known food writers.

The food has touches of California (the Morgans' previous home) and the Caribbean. The menu changes nightly and always features a vegetarian entrée.

One recent dinner started with Caribbean seafood gumbo, while another opened with smoked shrimp taco with chèvre and balsamic greens. There is always a choice of entrées (often four), including grilled lobster and shrimp with black bean salad, grilled quail with mango-strawberry vinaigrette and gingered veal scaloppini with brown pepper rice. Banana beach shortcake or piña colada cake are among the desserts.

You can order à la carte at The Sugar Mill as well.

There is a fixed price for the four-course meal. Menus are planned for a two-week period so you can check the menu for the night you'd like to dine here. Reservations for dinner are a must year-round. Casual chic attire.

Tortola

Brandywine Bay Restaurant
Brandywine Bay (three miles east of Road Town)
☎ (284) 495-2301
Expensive
Dinner only 6:30-9:30 pm
Closed Sunday

Watch for the sign that says Brandywine Bay Estates (right turn) and follow the narrow road past townhouses to a private house overlooking the channel. You dine on a cobblestoned garden terrace and the ambience, service and gourmet food combine to make this a superb experience. The chef creates all the sauces, dressings, soups and desserts and you can be sure that they are fresh because the menu changes daily.

Charter boats can anchor here overnight. Brandywine Bay is as elegant a restaurant as you can find on Tortola.

The Tuscan menu often includes beef or vegetarian carpaccio, mussels arrabbiata and homemade mozzarella. Entrées include roast duck with mango sauce, coconut-crusted rack of lamb with red Thai curry sauce and porcini-crusted ahi tuna. Tiramisu or the lemon tart finishes the meal with a bang. Brandywine Bay has an extensive wine list. You can peek at the temperature-controlled wine cellar. Reservations a must. Casual chic attire.

Eclipse

Penn's Landing Marina
Fat Hog's Bay, East End
☎ (284) 495-1646
Moderate-Expensive
Dinner 5-10 pm
Closed Sunday (Monday off-season)
Closed August

Eclipse is like the ugly duckling that becomes a beautiful swan. It's not much to look at, with only a dozen tables on a drab gray covered terrace at the marina's entrance. But the menu comes as quite a surprise. Its Asian-fusion and Caribbean dishes are exceptional and its chef has won many international awards.

You can spend an evening sampling small dishes on the two-page grazing menu. Favorites include tuna carpaccio, cracked calamari, scallop ceviche, coconut shrimp and fresh mussels. Heartier dishes include lobster ravioli, filet mignon, a variety of curries and shrimp tempura.

Eclipse has a take-out menu that includes house-made pizza.

The bar, always crowded, draws people from the marina, while the restaurant draws diners from all over the world. The owner/chef doesn't take himself too seriously. The sign at the entrance reads "Eclectic culinary delights and moonshine." The restaurant is very small so reservations are a must. Informal attire.

BVI Steak, Chop & Pasta House

Windy Hill (above Carrot Bay)

☎ (284) 494-5433

Moderate

Lunch & dinner, noon-9:30 pm

Closed Wednesdays

Location, location, location and the food is outstanding too. When BVI Steak House was located in Road Town it was a top dining option, but its new location overlooking Carrot and Cane Bays makes it unbeatable. Sunsets seem to last forever, so come for a drink before dinner. Owned by a transplanted New Yorker, this restaurant is both a steak house and an Italian eatery. The Italian specialties include several pastas with homemade sauces, lasagna, eggplant or chicken parmigiana, and shrimp scampi. Filet mignon, rib lamb chops or pork chops are served with a starch and vegetable. Starters include shrimp cocktail, bruschetta or tomato-onion salad. The garlic bread is made in-house. Try it. They serve wine by the glass and have a large cocktail menu. Reserve for dinner in season. Casual chic attire.

Le Cabanon

Waterfront Drive, Road Town

☎ (284) 494-8660

Expensive

Dinner from 6:30 pm; lunch from 11:30 weekdays

Closed Sunday

It's easy to miss Le Cabanon. It's a low-ceilinged patio eatery tucked under a cover of trees and dwarfed by the bustling Pusser's next door. But it has become a popular spot for both locals and visitors. While the food is French and formal, the atmosphere is relaxed and convivial. French onion soup or Caesar salad are good starters; then move on to the rib-eye steak, rack of lamb or the shepherd's pie, made with duck

Bistro-style dining and imbibing under the stars make for a lovely evening at Le Cabanon. Dress is casual.

Tortola

instead of beef. Chocolate or coconut mousse or a platter of French cheeses are good closers.

West Indian Restaurants

There are lots of small restaurants in Road Town and scattered throughout Tortola that list themselves as "West Indian" in government brochures. True, they have a few typical items on the menu, but the bulk of the choices are similar to those found on dinner menus in the US. A good rule of thumb is to avoid restaurants that serve all three meals. There are, however, a score of restaurants on the island specializing in West Indian fare that are highly regarded by locals and visitors. These are typically family-run, with the owner as chef and everyone else pitching in. Small (some have only a dozen tables), they offer al fresco dining on a patio or facing a beach strip and the décor is supplied by Mother Nature.

Reservations are a must since West Indian restaurants cook to the house. Typically inexpensive, the smaller ones often do not accept credit cards.

What are West Indian specialties? They include curries with chicken, beef, pork or goat. Stewed mutton, chicken, beef or goat are also very popular. Sauces are often tomato-based with lots of onions and, while spicy, they are not "hot." Conch in soup, with butter sauce or in fritters, is delicious, as is saltfish and fried local catches. Johnny cakes, fungi, barbecued ribs and meats are almost always on the menu. Don't be afraid to ask about the dishes before you order. Rotis have become very popular here since they can be eaten on the run rather like tacos. Rotis are thin bread wrapped around a filing of goat, conch, whelk or mutton with a creole-style sauce. They are delicious.

Above: Sailboat at dusk, Virgin Gorda (BVI Tourist Board)

Below: Woman at the Baths, Virgin Gorda (BVI Tourist Board)

The beaches of Virgin Gorda are seldom crowded (BVI Tourist Board)

Above: Snorkeling off Virgin Gorda (BVI Tourist Board)
Below: Palm tree at sunset, Virgin Gorda (BVI Tourist Board)

Above: Brewers Bay, Jost Van Dyke (www.walkwithremar.com)

Below: White Bay, Jost Van Dyke (www.imivi.com)

Above: Anegada, from the International Space Station

Below: Children on the beach, Anegada (BVI Tourist Board)

Above: Anegada lobster fisherman (BVI Tourist Board)

Below: Norman Island (Jim Scheiner, Voyages Ariane Travel)

Above: Iguana on Guana Island (BVI Tourist Board)
Below: Local girl on Guana (BVI Tourist Board)

Palm's Delight
Carrot Bay (North Shore)
☎ (284) 495-4863
Inexpensive
Dinner 6-10 pm
No credit cards

On the water's edge, this multicolored cottage sits between the town's two churches. It has a dozen plastic-covered tables on a covered terrace and a few others indoors. The chef/owner, Iona, plans her daily menu after visiting the local markets and fishermen. Her specialties include ginger chicken and sautéed shrimp. The crayfish with creole sauce is a personal favorite. Pâtés and rotis are available as well. Palm's Delight is arguably the island's best West Indian eatery.

Mrs. Scatliffe's Restaurant-Bar
Carrot Bay (North Shore)
☎ (284) 495-4556
Moderate
Dinner 7-9, lunch 12-2 weekdays
No credit cards

This is the most comfortable West Indian restaurant on the island. It's in the Scatliffe family's home. A flight of stone steps leads from the garden (where the fruits, vegetables and herbs are grown) to the second floor, where dinner is served. There are starched tablecloths, candles and flowers on each table and a great view of the water too. One of the daughters will seat you while her husband fixes you the best fruit daiquiri on the island. Although the menu varies, you can count on spiced papaya soup and coconut bread. Steaming hot chicken in coconut is served in the shell and curried goat, pot roast pork and Cornish hen are favorites. Desserts include coconut pie, soursop sherbet and tart lime pie.

Tortola

A lively fungi band often plays at dinner. You must reserve for dinner early in the day and that is when you order your food. Mrs. Scatliffe cooks only to the house count so you can't just drop in. Lunch is less formal.

Quitos' Gazebo
Cane Garden Bay (North Shore)
☎ (284) 495-4837
Moderate
Lunch & dinner 6:30-9:30
Closed Monday

Quito Rhymer is the BVI's most famous reggae singer. He is also an entrepreneur, owning both a popular beachfront restaurant and a boutique hotel (see page 74). The restaurant, on the beach, is an oversized beach shack with an indoor dining area and tables on the covered terrace. At night, there are candles on the tables and the service is slow and un-hurried. The menu is Caribbean, but with international touches. You can start with conch fritters or a roasted tomato-onion salad. Baby back ribs, steaks and piña colada chicken are popular entrées, as are blackened tuna with tropical salsa, and the seafood combo. Wednesday night is fish fry night, a traditional BVI affair, where the fish is grilled and the chicken barbecued. It includes salads and French fries for a set price. Sunday night is roti night.

You can't help but notice that the bar is the focal point of the restaurant. Many customers spend their evening at the bar enjoying the appetizers and beer. The treat is Quito Rhymer, who performs here solo on Tuesday and Thursday (from 8:30 pm) and with his reggae band, The Edge, on Friday and Saturday from 9:30. The reggae band plays without Quito when he is on tour. If you enjoy reggae music, pick up some of Quito's CDs. Informal.

Myett's Garden and Grill
Cane Garden Bay (North Shore)
☎ (284) 495-9649
Moderate-Inexpensive
Lunch & dinner

Nestled in the trees of Cane Garden Bay Beach, this is an upscale beach shack with tables on a covered terrace and on the beach itself. Because this is an extremely popular beach, the restaurant is jumping at lunch and at sunset happy hours. The lunch menu offers burgers, spicy wings, beer-battered shrimp, conch chowder and jerk chicken Caesar salads. Wraps and rotis are popular as well. Dinner features baby back ribs, seafood pasta, conch fritters, grilled steaks and chicken. Freshly grilled lobster served with salad is the house specialty. There is music most evenings and at Sunday brunch.

C&F Bar and Restaurant
Purcell Estate (near Wickham's Cay II), Road Town
☎ (284) 494-4941
Moderate
Dinner from 6:30-11

Chef Clarence Emmanuel won many culinary awards while working at several of Tortola's restaurants and his own place is now an award winner. Clarence makes the best barbecued ribs and chicken in town and the seafood is delicious too. A favorite here is crab and cucumber salad, and the fresh scallops in lime-butter sauce are a close second. Curried conch, grilled wahoo, curried coconut mutton and fried scallops are in demand. Informal.

No reservations, so sometimes there's a wait to be seated.

Tortola

Struggling Man's Place
Sea Cow Bay (near Nanny Cay)
☎ (284) 494-4163
Inexpensive
Serves lunch and dinner from 6:30-10 pm

This is a tiny spot with a great view of Drake's Channel and nearby islands. It serves curries, especially mutton and goat. Rotis, chicken and chips and stewed conch and lobster are delicious. .

Roti Palace
Russel Hill (off Main Street), Road Town
☎ (284) 494-4196
Inexpensive
Lunch only

A roti is a specialty of Trinidad and Guayana. Curries here include goat, whelk, conch, beef and chicken. Try some mango chutney as a condiment.

Other Restaurants in Road Town

Capriccio Di Mare
Waterfront Drive (near ferry deck), Road Town
☎ (284) 494-5369
Inexpensive
Breakfast 8-10:30
Open 11-9 pm
Closed Sunday

If there's a spot for people-watching on Tortola, Capriccio di Mare, an authentic Italian café and bar, is it. It is open from 8 am each morning and centrally located on Waterfront Drive. Virtually all of Tortola strolls by this sidewalk café. There are a dozen tables on the patio, as well as an indoor dining room. This informal spot is owned by Cele and Davide Pugliese, who also own the gourmet Italian eatery, Brandywine Bay (see page 83). Here they have kept the menu simple, but there is something to eat all day long and the food is carefully prepared. Pizza is a good choice for lunch or dinner. Thin-crusted, they are topped with tomatoes, mozzarella, anchovies, ham, sausages and grilled eggplant. The pastas are also excellent and there are over a dozen choices. If you want something lighter, try a glass of wine and a grilled ham and cheese sandwich on focaccia bread or a café latte and a crostini napoli (with anchovies and mozzarella). This is an informal spot and a very pleasant one.

Pusser's Pub
Waterfront Drive, Road Town
☎ (284) 494-2467
Inexpensive
Open 11 am-10 pm daily

You can't miss Pusser's. It's the multi-colored building with neatly mowed lawn that looks totally out of place on Waterfront Drive. Although it resembles an old fashioned general store in a small town in Kansas, you'll be pleased to discover – especially on a hot afternoon – that it's an air-conditioned bar/deli.

The menu includes pastrami, turkey and roast beef sandwiches, a variety of pizzas with a dozen topping choices and burgers and fries. The English dinner pies are tasty and, with a salad, make a filling meal. Try the shepherd's pie with ground beef and baked mashed potato topping or the chicken pie with asparagus and other vegetables. The food runs a poor second here to the popular bar that is always SRO. The pub is famous for the rum drinks that have celebrity names (made with Pusser's rum) and it is the Pusser's Painkiller in particular that cures all ills.

PUSSER'S PAINKILLER

It blends rum, cream of coconut, pineapple and orange juices over ice. Just one helps you forget all your disappointments.

The Captin's Table
Wickham's Cay I, Road Town
☎ (284) 494-3885
Moderate
Lunch 11-3 weekdays, dinner nightly from 6 pm
Closed Sundays off-season

The Captin's Table is an island fixture. The menu is international but French-leaning and delicious. There are small dining areas, all attractively decorated, or you can select a table on the terrace, which faces the harbor.

You can pick your lobster from the "lobster pool" that sits in the center of the dining room. The lunch menu has jerk duck, bangers and mash (sausage and mashed potatoes), Thai chicken satay and several pasta dishes. The dinner menu's dishes combine fresh local seafood and meats with light sauces and herbs. Look for duckling with berry sauce, traditional escargot, mussels provencale or rack of lamb with mint. Informal attire.

Spaghetti Junction
Inner Harbor Marina, Road Town
☎ (284) 494-4880
Moderate
Dinner 6-10, closed Sunday

Spaghetti Junction is a lively spot.

On the second level of a two-toned blue building near Wickham's Cay I, Spaghetti Junction will remind you of your neighborhood trattoria. It serves comfort food, Italian-style, and the ambience is relaxed and friendly. There are many nightly specials that include fresh local fish, but the dishes that combine pasta with seafood are best. Spinach lasagna, jambalaya pasta, snapper with curry or angel hair pasta and penne with spicy tomato sauce are delicious. The tables on the terrace face the harbor and marina. They're often filled with local yachtsmen and day-sail crews. Casual.

Virgin Queen
Fleming Street Roundabout, Road Town
☎ (284) 494-2310
Inexpensive
Hours 11 am-10 pm Mon-Fri, 6-10 pm Sat
Closed Sunday

Its main menu is a mix of West Indian and British fare but the ambience is all British pub, complete with dartboards. There are better places to eat West Indian food so stick to the shepherd's pie, bangers and mash and Virgin wings. The restaurant's signature dish is "Queen's Pizza," a crusty pie topped with cheese, sausage, onions, green peppers and mushrooms. The bar is noisy and crowded. It's fun.

Tortola

Snacks & Treats

The Courtyard Coffee Shop, Main Street, Road Town, is a tiny gingerbread-style house that serves Italian ice creams, coffee drinks and gourmet teas. Great pastries. Hours 7:30-5:30 Mon-Fri, 7:30-1 Saturday .

Road Town Bakery, Main Street, sells freshly made bread, rolls, muffins and pastries, as well as coffee and tea for take-out. Hours 7-1; closed Sunday.

Nature's Way, Mill Mall, Road Town, is a health food store that sells vegetarian dishes for take-out or to eat in the dining area. Menu changes daily. Hours 8-5; closed Sunday.

La Dolce Vita, Waterfront Drive, Road Town, sells ice creams, with their specialty being Italian ice creams. They also offer ices and low-fat ice creams. Hours 11-8.

Dining With a View

Skyworld
Ridge Road (northwest of Road Town)
☎ (284) 494-3567
Inexpensive-Expensive
Lunch 11-2:30; dinner 6:30-10:30

The view from Skyworld's terrace is stunning, both by day and at night. It encompasses a wide swath of the Sir Francis Drake Channel, many of the islands in the channel, plus the entire Road Town area.

Reservations a must for dinner. Casual chic attire.

The food is very good too, as a posted review from *Gourmet Magazine* will attest. If you choose to eat lunch here, ask for a table on the outside terrace. The lunch menu is heavy on burgers and sandwiches but does have some Caribbean specialties such as conch fritters, lobster casserole and black bean soup. Dinner finds a continental menu, including filet mignon with port, fresh fish with tarragon beurre blanc and chicken stuffed with sausage. Key lime pie seems to be the dessert of choice.

> **Note:** Skyworld is adjacent to a scenic stop also called Skyworld so you can pull over to see the view without eating.

West End Dining Spots

Pusser's Landing
Soper's Hole Marina, West End
☎ (284) 495-4554
Inexpensive-Moderate
Lunch 11-3, dinner 6-10

A casual spot for a relaxed, informal light dinner or lunch, Pusser's Landing is in the marina and shopping center at Soper's Hole. It's a two-level nautical restaurant with umbrella-shaded tables on an open patio and a more formal second-level dining room. Lunch is served on the patio and includes lobster club sandwiches, burgers, rotis and fish n' chips British-style (fried in beer batter and served with vinegar). Wings, conch fritters and a variety of pizzas are served at lunch and all afternoon. The menu here includes peel n' eat shrimp, steaks, local fish and chicken. The bar has a large satellite TV and stays open late. Try a Pusser's coffee with rum and whipped cream. It's a great sleep inducer.

Peg Leg Landing
Nanny Cay Marina (West End)
☎ (284) 494-4895
Moderate

Although not an attractive building from the outside (weathered shingles with a blue and yellow awning), Peg Leg Landing's dining areas are a very pleasant surprise. A long bar, thick wooden tables, stained glass windows and comfortable rattan-backed chairs make for an inviting atmosphere. The menu emphasizes local seafood, including lobster, steaks, pasta and pizza. There are specials nightly and always a vegetarian choice. Perched on stilts near the water, Peg Leg Landing has a very popular bar scene. Add to that the terrace pool, and you can see why it's a busy spot from the 11:30 am opening well into Happy Hour at 4:30-7 pm. Dinner starts at 7. Nanny Cay has recently changed ownership and has been totally upgraded. The marina is very successful and there are now some good shops here as well.

Jolly Roger Inn
Soper's Hole, West End
☎ (284) 495-4559
Moderate
Hours 8 am-midnight
Closed August 15-October 1

Jolly Roger stands next to the port, where the ferries from the US Virgin Islands land. It's easy to overlook because the area is so quiet and all the action on the West End is across the bridge at the marina. The inn has five guest rooms and the restaurant serves three meals daily. If you are staying nearby, you can enjoy the food, which draws from Caribbean, Pan-Asian and Tuscan cuisines, including pizzas. The weekend barbecue is popular and has live music. Informal.

East End Dining

The Secret Garden
Josiah's Bay
☎ (284) 495-1834
Inexpensive
All-day menu, noon-10 pm (closed Tuesday)

This is a charming café is set in the courtyard of an 18th-century Greathouse, Josiah's Bay Plantation. The mini-complex also houses an art gallery and a craft store. The food served is light, with many salads offered as main courses. Sandwiches, on homemade bread, include an Asian tuna burger and a lamb gyro. A dish that many diners share is the chickpea and artichoke hummus served with Secret Garden pita. Other entrées include gourmet pizzas, beef sate with peanut sauce, flying fish pie and sautéed snapper with papaya sauce. The desserts, all made here, are fabulous. Peanut butter pie, homemade carrot cake and the frozen chocolate fudge cake are all winners.

Josiah's Bay is on Tortola's North Shore and on the island's east end, which is the least-developed part of the island. The road leading here is steep and unlit, so we recommend you come for lunch and then judge for yourself whether you want to deal with a night drive.

Fat Hog Bob's
Hodges Creek, Maya Cove
☎ (284) 495-1010
Inexpensive-Moderate
All-day menu from 11 am

Fat Hog Bob's is not a gourmet eatery but it is one of
the island's most popular restaurants because the
food is delicious, the portions are huge and it is inexpensive. There is a very large dining room with
widely spaced tables, comfortable couches, hanging
hammocks and a large-screen satellite TV that
shows major sporting events from Britain and the
US. There are tables on the open-air terrace that
sits just above the water.

The lunch menu is heavy on burgers, barbecued ribs
and chicken, reuben sandwiches and spinach and
Caesar salads. The dinner menu serves all of the
above but adds porterhouse steaks, grilled shrimp,
lobsters and fresh fish. Bananas Foster and mud
cakes are popular desserts. The bar's high-back di-
rectors' chairs are always occupied.

*Reserve for
dinner, espe-
cially if
there's a
major sport-
ing event.*

Harbor View Restaurant
Harbor View Marina
Fat Hog's Bay
☎ (284) 495-2797
Inexpensive
Lunch & dinner, 11:30 am-10 pm

One of the few restaurants on Tortola that would
blend into a Stateside location, Harbor View is a
second-level spot overlooking a marina. Its large
contemporary dining room has widely spaced,
highly polished tables and colorful prints. There are
also tables on the open terrace. The lunch menu is
best, with stuffed deli sandwiches, meatball subs,
turkey melts, a variety of wraps, quesadillas, burgers and pizza. The dinner menu is French, including duck breast with blueberry compote and

fennel-rubbed rack of lamb. It's expensive, so you might want to stick to lunch here.

After Dark

 Tortola wakes up early to catch the first rays of sunshine and the first breeze over the channel. The island tucks in early, too, and what nightlife there is revolves around the hotels and restaurants. There are reggae bands and calypso groups, a mellow guitar, some jazz and fungi (scratch bands, traditional here).

SCRATCH BAND MUSIC

Also known as quelbe and quadrille, this is an indigenous, grass-roots folk music that originated in the US Virgin Islands and has spread to other parts of the Caribbean. Lyrics immortalize historical events, spread gossip, or reflect on daily life. The musicians play homemade instruments – from car muffler pipes, to a banjo made from a sardine can.

There are evening cruises. Keep in mind that some hotel rooms do not have a TV set, although they often have a communal set that has cable. Check at your hotel activity desk for special dinner events such as a poolside barbecue or West Indian buffet.

There is a movie theater in Road Town. Pick up a copy of **Limin' Times**, a free weekly entertainment guide distributed at hotels, restaurants and the Tourist Kiosk. It contains schedules.

Live Music & Special Events

The Last Resort, on Bellamy Cay (off Beef Island), has buffet dinner followed by owner Tony Snell's cabaret act-patter and songs. Other artists sometimes perform. Reservations required. ☎ (284) 495-2520. Use the "hotline" phone at the dock in Trellis Bay to call for the ferry (it does so automatically when you pick it up).

Quito's Gazebo is owned by Quito Rhymer, a popular island folk and reggae singer, who plays guitar solo on Tuesdays and Thursdays and with his band "Quito and the Edge" on Fridays and Saturdays. When Quito is touring, other groups play. ☎ (284) 495-4837. Cane Garden Bay Beach.

Bomba's Shack, in Apple Bay, is an island favorite and famous for its monthly "full-moon" parties, which spill over onto the beach and the empty lot across the road. Island bands on Sunday and Wednesday night. You can't miss it. It's a beachfront shack decorated with everything but the kitchen sink. ☎ (284) 495-4148.

Myett's, on Cane Garden Bay Beach, is a terraced beachfront restaurant well known for its Sunday barbecue lunch that lasts for hours. The music starts at lunch and continues into the night. Local bands play Friday, Saturday, Sunday and Monday nights. ☎ (284) 495-9543.

North Shore Shell Museum, Carrot Bay, has a fungi band every night but Sunday. It's near several West Indian restaurants. ☎ (284) 495-4714.

The Pub, Fort Burt Marina, Road Town, has Happy Hour every night, dart boards, lively customers and music on several nights a week. Usually blues or jazz. ☎ (284) 494-2608.

Tortola

Pusser's Road Town Pub, on the waterfront in Road Town, is a popular meeting spot for charter boat people. Their special event nights, such as Ladies' Night or Nickel Beer Night, keep the place crowded. ☎ 494-2467.

Pusser's Landing Soper's Hole (West End) has live bands several nights a week, shows major sporting events on a large-screen TV and serves terrific pizza. ☎ (284) 495-4554.

Bing's Drop Inn, Fat Hog's Bay (East End), has a DJ every night except Monday. ☎ (284) 495-2627.

Jolly Roger Inn, West End Ferry Dock, has live entertainment on Friday and Saturday evenings. ☎ (284) 495-4559.

Da Loose Mongoose, Trellis Bay (Beef Island), often has a blues singer on Sunday nights. ☎ (284) 495-2303.

Cane Garden Bay Beach is home to small night spots that draw local crowds, as well as the larger Quito's Gazebo and Myett's, mentioned previously. Check out **Big Banana** and **Elm's Beach Bar**. They often have music under the stars.

Sebastian's Seaside Grill, Little Apple Bay, has dancing under the stars and some of the island's best bands on weekends. ☎ (284) 495-4212.

Fat Hog Bob's, Maya Cove, East End, has special event nights and a giant TV screen tuned to major sporting events. ☎ (284) 495-1010.

Tortola A-Z

Practicalities

 ATM MACHINE: Barclay's at Soper's Hole Marina accepts Cirrus, MC/VISA and Plus cards.

BANKS: They are clustered on Wickham's Cay I, Road Town. Hours are Mon-Thurs 9 am-2:30 pm, Friday 9 am-2:30 pm, 4:30-6 pm. Major banks include **Barclay's**, **Chase**, **Scotia BVI Ltd.**, and **First Caribbean Bank**.

EMERGENCY NUMBERS: Police, fire, ambulance, dial 999 or 911.

GASOLINE: Price runs between $2.50 and $3 a gallon. There are gas stations on **Waterfront Drive**, both East and West of Road Town.

HEALTH CARE: **Peebles Hospital**, Road Town, ☎ (284) 494-3497; **Eureka Medical Clinic**, Road Town, ☎ (284) 494-2346.

ICE CREAM STORES: **Gourmet Ice Cream & Drinks**, Soper's Hole Marina; **La Dolce Vita**, Waterfront Drive.

NEWSPAPERS: There are three weekly newspapers. Total weekly circulation is about 2,000 for all three. The *Island Sun*, the oldest newspaper in the BVI, is published on Fridays and is available online at www.islandsun.com. The *BVI Beacon*, the second oldest newspaper, is published on Thursdays (online at www.bvibeacon.com). The *BVI Stand Point*, the newest, is published on Tuesdays (www.bvistandpoint.com). In addition, there is *Limin' Times*, a weekly entertainment guide. Daily newspapers from the USVI arrive each afternoon. **Esme's** shop in the plaza (across from the ferry dock) usually has them.

PHARMACIES: **JR O'Neal Ltd.**, Main Street (near Post Office), ☎ (284) 494-2292; **B&F Medical Complex**, Mill Mall, Wickham's Cay I, ☎ (284) 494-2196.

POST OFFICE: The main branch is on Main Street near the plaza. Hours are Mon-Fri 9 am-4 pm, Sat 9 am-noon. There are branches at East End, West End, Carrot Bay and Cane Garden Bay.

BVI stamps are particularly attractive.

PUBLIC LIBRARY: On Main Street, it has a large selection of books about the Caribbean and local history. Tourists can borrow books.

PUSSER'S RUM: For 285 years, from 1685 to 1970, a daily lot of Pusser's Rum was issued to British sailors at noon. It was never sold or offered to the public till 1980 when permission to sell it was granted by the Admiralty. The Royal Navy Sailor's Fund receives a donation for each bottle sold. For sale at Pusser's shops in Road Town, Soper's Hole and Marina Cay.

SPEED BUMPS: There are scores of speed bumps on Tortola's roads. They mark residential areas. The speed limit is 20 mph in these areas, which is very good because the bumps are not brightly marked and very easy to miss till you go over one. Also be conscious of the goats, sheep and occasional roosters wandering beside the road, particularly on North Shore Road.

VISAR: Virgin Island Search and Rescue is an organization dedicated to saving lives at sea. Founded in 1988, after the drowning of several school children, they have answered thousands of distress calls and saved hundreds of lives. Donations are appreciated. www.visar.org, ☎ (284) 494-4357.

WINES & SPIRITS: **Caribbean Cellars**, Port Purcell, east of Road Town; **Tico**, Wickham's Cay II.

Spas & Beauty Salons

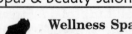

Wellness Spa & Salon, Long Bay Beach Hotel, ☎ (284) 495-4252, manicures, pedicures, facials and massages. Outcalls.

Oasis Salon & Spa, Village Cay Hotel, 3rd Floor, ☎ (284) 494-8891, hair care, facials, waxing, manicures, pedicures. Outcalls.

Calabash Fitness Centre, Prospect Reef
☎ (284) 494-3311, massages, facials.

Specialty Food Shops

 Whether provisioning a yacht or stocking the kitchen of your villa, you'll find what you need at the shops below:

Ample Hamper, Wickham's Cay I, Soper's Hole, Hodge's Creek Marina.

Best of British, Mill Mall, Wickham's Cay, sells food, beverages, newspapers and magazines from Britain.

Riteway Market, Road Reef Plaza (west of Road Town).

Small Islands Near Tortola

Pusser's Marina Cay

Marina Cay, a tiny island set behind a sheltered lagoon, is a tropical six-acre oasis in Trellis Bay, off Beef Island. Several years ago Pusser's Company bought the cay and renovated and refurbished the small hotel on it.

Pusser's Marina Cay
Box 626, Road Town, Tortola
☎ (284) 494-2174
www.pussers.com

The hotel's four rooms and two villas can accommodate 16-20 guests so it's pretty much a private hide-away. In fact, you can rent the entire island for a special event. All the accommodations face water. You can scuba dive nearby, sail small boats, windsurf, kayak and snorkel. You'll dine at the water's edge on West Indian and international special-

Tortola

ties, including lobster. There's a small Pusser's Company Store selling resort wear and rums. You can enjoy a drink at the Cay's Summit and have a 360° view of neighboring islands. The original owner of Marina Cay, Rob White, wrote a book called *Our Island* about his experiences that became a film.

Marina Cay is a popular anchorage for yachts so many of their guests will join you for lunch and dinner. It's only 10 minutes by launch from Marina Cay to the Government Dock on Trellis Bay, Beef Island, so it's easy to go to Da Loose Mongoose for dinner (see page 100) or even into Road Town.

You can visit Marina Cay for the day by taking the launch from Trellis Bay on Beef Island. You'll have to pay for watersports gear, lounges and the launch.

Cooper Island

Hotels such as Mooring's Mariner's Inn and Treasure Isle in Road Town, that do not have beach access, run ferry service to Cooper Island daily. It's free to their guests, but you can hop on for a fee. The ferry leaves from their dock on Wickham's Cay II. A visit to Cooper Island makes a terrific day-trip.

Cooper Island, just a few minutes from Road Town by ferry, houses a few private homes and the Cooper Island Beach Club.

Cooper Island Beach Club
Parlmes Enterprises,
Box 512, Turner's Falls, MA 01376
☎ (800) 542-4624
www.cooper-island.com

The rustic beach club has 12 rooms, neatly but basically furnished with ceiling fans, but no telephones or TVs. Electricity is scarce so they frown on use of electric appliances. All rooms do have private baths.

DON'T TOUCH!

The club sits on Machioneel Bay, which is named for the poisonous apple trees that grow there. Avoid touching them and certainly don't eat the fruit.

The waters here are incredibly clear and you can see the sandy bottom covered in sea grass. The club organizes scuba trips and there is good snorkeling at Cistern Point, on the southern edge of the beach. The club's very informal restaurant serves lunch and dinner with West Indian and international specialties. There is often a barbecue.

There are no roads on the island, but you can hike the marked trail to the top of a nearby hill. It's only a 15-minute walk, but take some water along since it can get quite hot. Road Town looks like a leisurely swim away across the channel.

Cooper Island Hideaways
1920 Barg Lane
Cincinnati, Ohio 45230
☎ (513) 2323-4126
www.cooperisland.com

Nearby are two beachfront cottages owned by a couple from Ohio. These are for rent fully furnished. There's a one-bedroom and a two-bedroom unit. They are expensive and extremely private.

Cooper Island has 20 moorings. They are almost always full so must be reserved in advance. Boats are required to be anchored by sunset and must stay overnight, so crew and guests often have dinner at the club.

Bellamy Cay

The Last Resort is a rollicking place set on a tiny islet in the middle of a stunning circular bay. There are no accommodations, but the restaurant/night spot is a lot of fun. The restaurant serves dinner nightly from 6:30-9:30. The English buffets have been replaced by a new menu that features fresh local fish, tapas and fusion cuisine. There are still a few old favorites like bangers and mash, but spicy Asian duck, BBQ ribs and chicken and tuna in mango salsa are new offerings. The bar opens at 11:30 am and light foods are available for those who come to the Cay for the swimming and watersports. After dinner there is a show with such characters as Vanilla the Donkey and the Singing Dogs. Owner Tony Snell takes over with a sharp wit and patter. Call ☎ (284) 495-2520 to make a reservation for dinner. The free ferry will pick you up at the Trellis Bay jetty on Beef Island.

Virgin Gorda

After claiming and naming hundreds of islands and cays for Spain, Columbus must have been weary of the task when he arrived here. Virgin Gorda translates to Fat Virgin.

As you fly over the island en route to the tiny seaside airstrip, you'll notice that Virgin Gorda is two distinct islands joined by a narrow ribbon of land. The northern part is mountainous, while the southern part is quite flat. The latter area, dubbed The Valley, has the island's largest village, Spanish Town, and its major attraction, The Baths. These, a remarkable arrangement of huge boulders on a stunning beach, have fallen in such a way as to create unique grottoes and coves, which you can snorkel or wade through.

The Baths are not the only great beach on Virgin Gorda. There are at least 20 others, some of which are virgin strips, accessible only by boat or by climbing down a fairly steep hill. As you drive around the island, you'll notice that, while the vegetation is lush and colorful flowers grow everywhere, it is all low to the ground. There are lots of cactus plants as well. That is due to the sparse rainfall, which, while a boon to vacationers, does create a severe water shortage.

The northern portion of the island has several tiny settlements and is much more mountainous than the south. Virgin Gorda Peak, which you can climb, stands at 1,370 feet. Several hotels are located on the peninsula that curves around North Sound. These are inaccessible by land and can be reached only by water taxis.

If you are surprised that these posh resorts have no road access, take a second to consider that, until the

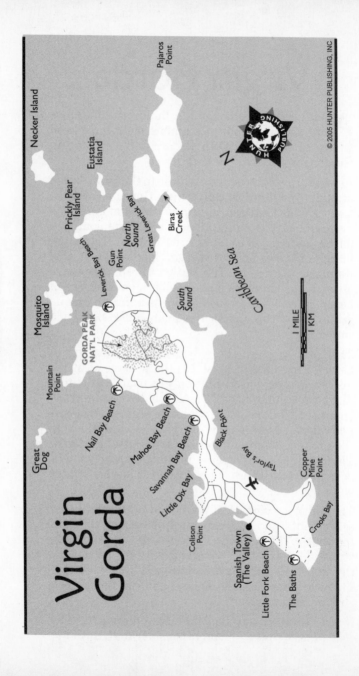

1950s, Virgin Gorda had not a single paved road, no telephones, no electricity, and no medical services. The few hundred people living here had to send their children to high school on Tortola.

Change came in 1961, when ground was broken for a resort on Little Dix Bay. Laurence Rockefeller spied this inlet while sailing nearby. He envisioned the property as a kind of wilderness beach and the resort he fashioned remains a 500-acre retreat where privacy and solitude are prized. The resort spurred the development of the Virgin Gorda Yacht Harbor and the airstrip.

Virgin Gorda is once again in the throes of dramatic change. An enormous building boom is underway with new villa communities being constructed at bays and coves throughout the island, while older communities are adding accommodations and amenities. The villas are being sold to individual buyers and then will be rental units managed by the development. There are no new hotels being built so most visitors to the island will stay in a villa. To reach these developments, new roads have been constructed and many restaurants have opened to serve the larger number of visitors.

While the physical character of the island is changing noticeably, Virgin Gorda's lure is still its natural beauty and the friendly, proud people who live here.

Getting There

By Air

There are no non-stop flights to Virgin Gorda from the US or Canada. The island's 3,000-foot seaside airstrip can service only commuter-size planes and helicopters. Most visitors fly to San Juan, Puerto

Rico or St. Thomas, USVI and transfer to small planes for the 40-minute flight (San Juan) or 20-minute flight (St. Thomas). The major US carriers to Puerto Rico include American Airlines, United, Continental, US Airways and Jet Blue. All except Jet Blue also fly to St. Thomas.

Air Sunshine, ☎ (800) 327-8900, has one daily flight from San Juan and one daily flight from St. Thomas, to Virgin Gorda.

Air St. Thomas, ☎ (284) 495-5935, has one flight from San Juan and one from St. Thomas every day but Sunday.

Check your baggage to your initial stop and then recheck it. Delayed baggage is common here.

Since these are very small planes, they fill up quickly, so you should make these reservations when you book your initial flight.

Because there are several flights daily from San Juan and St. Thomas to Tortola's Beef Island Airport, most visitors fly there and take a ferry to Virgin Gorda. (See page 32 for details)

By Sea

Tortola - Virgin Gorda

Speedy's, ☎ (284) 495-5240, and **Smith's Ferry Services**, ☎ (284) 495-4495, both have a half-dozen ferries from Road Town, Tortola to Virgin Gorda daily. They each have three ferries on Sunday. They stagger the time schedules so you can count on a dozen crossings daily.

The **North Sound Express**, ☎ (284) 495-5240, is based in Virgin Gorda. It has ferries on Tuesday, Thursday and Saturday that leave from St. Thomas, make a stop in Road Town, Tortola, then continue on to Virgin Gorda. Most ferries from St. Thomas require a stop in Tortola to pass through customs and then a separate ferry from Tortola to Virgin Gorda. There are a score of crossings each day. (See *St. Thomas-Tortola*, page 31)

Entry Requirements

A valid passport or some proof of citizenship (driver's license, birth certificate) plus a current photo ID is required for entry to the BVI. At your first BVI stop, you will fill out a Tourist Information form, half of which will be collected on entry and the other half when you depart. Departure tax is $10 for air travelers and $5 for those leaving by sea.

Getting Around

On Land

There is no public transportation on the island and you will have to rely on taxis, unless you rent a car or jeep.

The companies below offer pick-up and drop-off services.

Island Style Jeep & Car Rentals, ☎/fax (284) 495-6300

L&S Jeep Rental & Taxi Service, ☎ (284) 495-5297, l&scarrentals@surfbvi.com

Mahogany Car Rentals, ☎ (284) 495-5469, mahoganycarrentals@surfbvi.com

3P Scooter Rental, ☎ (284) 495-6870

Driving Tips

 To rent a car/jeep on Virgin Gorda, you must be 21 years of age and hold a valid driver's license. You will be issued a temporary BVI license for a $10 fee. Remember to drive on the left. There are few cars here.

The main road, North Sound Road, connects Spanish Town in the south with Leverick Bay and Gun Creek on North Sound. It is paved but pitted. New roads have been built to allow access to recently built villa communities.

On Water

 Travel around North Sound is on the water. Water taxis, ferries and resort-operated motorboats link Biras Creek Resort, Bitter End Yacht Club and other islands in the Sound to the mainland. Virtually all leave from the dock in Gun Creek.

Free ferries connect Gun Creek and the Bitter End Yacht Club. They run on the half-hour starting at 6:30 am, with the last ferry at 10:30 pm. Return ferries run on the hour starting at 6 am and stopping at 11 pm.

Saba Rock Resort also offers service from Gun Creek. It is primarily for guests, but visitors can use it if they have dining reservations. Call for schedule, ☎ (284) 495-7711.

You can rent a Boston Whaler or small motorboat and cross the Sound or head to one of the little islands nearby. Rentals are available at Leverick Bay Resort, ☎ (284) 495-7421, or The Bitter End, ☎ (284) 494-2745, (800) 872-2392.

Island Taxi Tours

If you decide to visit the island just for the day, consider calling **African Pride Taxi Service**. Ask for Cumba. He loves the island and knows every inch of it. ☎ (284) 495-6091 or africanpride@sufbvi.com.

Orientation

For such a small island (8.1 square miles), Virgin Gorda has three geographically distinct areas.

The South

The southern end of Virgin Gorda is flat and strewn with giant boulders. It is home to **Spanish Town**, the island's capital and the area where most islanders live. The island's most famous site, **The Baths**, is located here as well. The Baths is a great beach on the southwest coast where the boulders have fallen in such a way as to create offshore caves and quiet pools to snorkel and swim through. Other beaches nearby are part of a national park. Home to Little Dix Bay Resort and several villa communities, the southern end of Virgin Gorda is called **The Valley**.

The Central Strip

Connected to the south by a strip of land that is only one mile wide at some spots, the central part of Virgin Gorda was best known for **Virgin Gorda Peak and National Park**. It soars to 1,370 feet and can be climbed. Now, several new communities have opened on the western coast and new roads leading to them have opened up a score of beaches that were previously accessible by water or rocky trails.

The North

The northern portion has developed around a stunning body of water called **North Sound**. It houses several small islands – some inhabited and others uninhabited but with anchorages. The southern coast of North Sound is home to **Leverick Bay Resort** and the tiny settlement of **Gun Creek**. Water taxis leave from Gun Creek for the resort hotels on North Sound's northern arm. **Biras Creek** and **The Bitter End Yacht Club** are accessible only by boat. The North Sound area is beautiful.

> **Note:** Virgin Gorda gets less rain than Tortola and therefore has less tropical vegetation. Some parts of the island are quite dry and you'll see cactus and scrub brush.

From Sunup to Sundown

 Because the resorts here offer so many enjoyable daytime activities, it is easy to spend your entire vacation on their grounds, and in their waters. But that would be a mistake. Put aside some time to explore Virgin Gorda and to meet the really nice people who live here.

North Sound Road, which runs from Spanish Town in the south to Leverick Bay on Gun Creek in the north, is Virgin Gorda's main road. It slices through the center of the island, offering stunning views of nearby islands. It passes virtually every interesting stop on the island and, since the island is so small, travel time between points is minimal. New roads have been constructed to permit access to the new villa communities springing up on bays and coves along Virgin Gorda's craggy coast. These also give easy access to lovely, pristine beaches that were previously accessible only by boat or by hiking along rocky paths.

Virgin Gorda's dive operators are well organized and scuba trips to nearby wrecks and reefs take place daily year-round. You can join a day-sail trip to nearby islands, where you can snorkel and sightsee. You can rent your own boat and visit small islands in North Sound or off the coast of Virgin Gorda. Many have fine beaches, beach shack eateries and anchorages. There is horseback riding, a mini-golf course, some good shops and a historic coppermine to explore. You can hike to the top of Virgin Gorda Peak or along the trails that connect The Baths to beaches at nearby national parks.

We'll start in Spanish Town, the capital of Virgin Gorda.

Virgin Gorda

Exploring Spanish Town & the Valley

Spanish Town, in The Valley, is the largest settlement on Virgin Gorda and most of the island's 3,000 residents live here. There are smaller settlements nearby and one at North Sound. Spanish Town was the capital of the BVI when the Spanish controlled it and worked the coppermine nearby. Now it's a tiny West Indian town with only a handful of streets.

Virgin Gorda Yacht Harbour is the hub of town. Its marina is a modern facility with slips for 120 yachts. There is a large provisioning shop and a liquor store, plus a dozen shops and restaurants in the adjoining shopping center. Check out the community bulletin board in the courtyard. It lists interesting island events such as fish fries and cricket matches that you can attend. Nearby, you'll see a cream-colored building with a flagpole. This is head-

The BVI Tourist Office is in the Yacht Harbour. They have island maps and printed materials you'll find helpful.

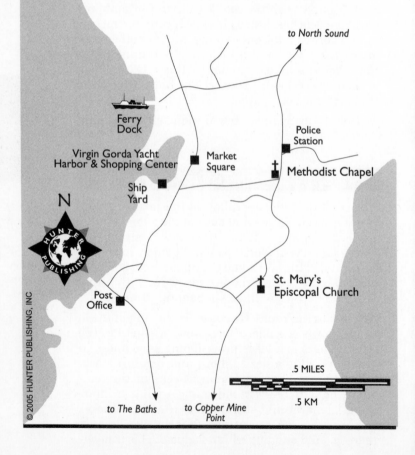

Spanish Town & The Valley

to North Sound

Ferry Dock

Virgin Gorda Yacht Harbor & Shopping Center

Police Station

Market Square

Methodist Chapel

Ship Yard

N

HUNTER PUBLISHING

St. Mary's Episcopal Church

Post Office

.5 MILES

.5 KM

to The Baths

to Copper Mine Point

quarters for the **Royal Virgin Islands Police**. In addition to their law enforcement tasks, they also serve as the local fire company.

Just north of the Yacht Harbour (near the ferry dock), you'll see a small beach shaded by seagrape trees. Adjacent to it is a historic **graveyard** where 10 graves offer a reminder of the early inhabitants of Virgin Gorda. The 18th-century tombs were built of red brick, stone, coral and lime plaster in a traditional manner. One grave, that of Susannah Frett, added in 1760, is unique. It is square and covered with carved inscriptions.

The road from town leads to the small airport, which was built by the Little Dix Bay Hotel Corp. North of the airport you'll see the **Methodist Chapel** (on Crab Hill Road). It is the oldest surviving building on the island. A simple masonry structure, it has arched windows and is topped by an elaborate roof. In existence since 1823, the chapel has been repaired and altered over time. During the 19th century, worshippers from nearby St. Thomas (which was Danish at the time) joined the congregation here. In the churchyard, the foundation of an old mission house is visible, as is a very old cemetery. The graves span three centuries. Note the piles of conch shells at the gravesites. Some islanders believe these shells have special powers that drive away evil spirits. The island's only health facility – a clinic – is nearby.

The church beyond it is **St. Mary's Episcopal Church**, built in 1875. In colonial times, Anglicanism was the official religion of the islands. This stone and brick building replaced an earlier wooden church that was destroyed by a hurricane. Inside the church, a copy of the consecration certificate is on display. Here too you'll see historic gravestones and conch shells near many traditional graves. The

building across Church Hill Road is the **Virgin Island Community Center**. A school during the day,
it is also a social center where islanders meet to celebrate holidays and other social events.

Another interesting stop in The Valley, south of the
airport, **Copper Mine Point** is the site of an abandoned coppermine and smelter. English adventurers
recorded the discovery of copper veins here in 1724,
but it is believed that the Spanish mined the area
earlier. The substantial ruins that remain today are
part of buildings constructed by a Cornish mining
company in the 19th century. The miners from
Cornwall England hired local people to work the
mine. When it was abandoned, the island reverted
to an agricultural economy.

The approach road is not paved and is bumpy even
for a jeep, but the views are so beautiful that it's
worth it. The stack and mill stand on a promontory
jutting into the sea. It is the easternmost point in
the BVI and part of the national park.

> **Note:** Little restoration has been done so
> the area is unstable. Tread lightly. Stop at
> The Mine Shaft, near the point, for a drink
> at sunset.

Exploring North Sound

Virgin Gorda's main road links Spanish Town to
North Sound Settlement, a mini-version of Spanish
Town. The road forks left to Leverick Bay Resort. At
the crossroads is the **O'Neal School**, one of two primary schools on the island. It wasn't until the late
1970s that a secondary school was built. Until then
the older students had to go to high school on
Tortola.

The right fork leads to **Gun Creek Jetty**, which is an important link between The Valley and the hotels on North Sound. Supplies and passengers are shuttled by water taxi from Gun Creek to Biras Creek, The Bitter End and other islands in the Sound. You can have lunch or dinner at one of the hotels above. Make reservations for dinner and the hotel ferry will meet you.

North Sound was once said to be big enough to hold all of the British Navy. Today its protected waters offer shelter to as many as 100 chartered yachts. North Sound offers unsurpassed sailing, deserted islands and cays to explore, colorful and unique wildlife for the naturalist and spectacular coral reefs for the diver. It also houses three resort hotels.

Beaches

The Baths

The most distinctive landmark in the BVI, The Baths resembles a disgruntled giant's building blocks. Imagine the frustrated giant tossing the gigantic boulders into the air. They fell haphazardly on and near the sandy beach, some remaining erect, while others toppled against each other. Actually, the unique boulder formations (boulders are scattered throughout the island) were created by an ancient volcanic upheaval. Over millions of years the jagged granite blocks have weathered into the smooth boulders visible today.

The boulders have fallen in such a way as to create grottos and seaside caves. Some have sunlight streaming through the cracks between rocks, others are open to bright sunlight, while others are eerily dark.

Virgin Gorda

Getting to The Baths is a lot of the fun. It is part of a string of beaches on Virgin Gorda's southwest coast. It is only five minutes by car from Spanish Town (you can sail to the area and anchor offshore) and an easy 20-minute stroll. Look for the roadside parking area that is home to The Top of the Baths and Mad Dog's eateries as well as a gift shop. Head to the adjacent path that leads downhill to the beach. Shaded, it winds 1,050 feet along a well-defined if rocky path. It takes about 15 minutes and you'll be joined by lizards, birds and butterflies.

There are no dangerous snakes in the BVI.

Many visitors arrive at the beach on dinghies from boats anchored offshore. The Baths is a popular stop for day-sail trips.

The beach has lockers and a small beach shack selling cold drinks and hot dogs, but no watersports rentals. Bring your own blanket and snorkeling gear.

Note: The National Parks Trust purchased the six acres that comprise The Baths from a local family in 1990. It is not officially part of Devil's Bay National Park, but is part of the 682-acre area that is protected by the Trust. The park encircles The Baths and paths have been cleared to join all the beach areas.

Devil's Bay National Park

The southwest coast of Virgin Gorda has beautiful white cedar trees, turpentine trees with red shiny bark and frangipani trees, as well as 20-foot cactus. Birds include doves, hummingbirds and bananaquits.

Devil's Bay National Park was established in 1964. It includes Little Fort, Big Trunk Bay, Little Trunk Bay, The Crawl, Spring Bay and Devil's Bay (south of The Baths). It also includes the Coppermine ruins and small offshore islands such as Fallen Jerusalem, Broken Jerusalem and Round Rock.

Little Fort is closest to Spanish Town. It is not a beach but is instead made up of piles of massive boulders covered by interesting flora. The old fort that stood there has crumbled away. The area, comprised of 36 acres, is a wildlife sanctuary.

The **Trunk Bays** and **Spring Bay** have lovely coral sand beaches. Spring Bay is the most attractive of the three. It too has huge boulders that make snorkeling attractive and is less crowded than The Baths. The lawn is popular with picnickers.

The Crawl can be reached along a coconut palm-lined path from Spring Bay. It is a natural boulder enclosure once used by fishermen as a corral to keep captured turtles and fish alive. It is an excellent snorkeling spot for beginners.

Devil's Bay has crystal-clear waters and a white sandy beach that is shaded by seagrape trees. It has no watersports rentals, so bring your own gear and food.

Fallen Jerusalem, **Broken Jerusalem** and **Round Rock** islands provide nesting sites for seabirds such as red-billed and white-tailed tropicbirds, brown boobies, terns, brown pelicans and laughing gulls. Goats once grazed on Fallen Jerusalem but no longer. All three are uninhabited and easily reached by boat.

You can walk from Devil's Bay to The Baths along a trail that starts at the beach and moves over and around huge granite boulders. You'll have to crawl at points, climb ladders at others and wade through water at still others. It takes about 20 minutes and edges saltwater grottos and ponds. There are no written signs, but small rock piles are used to point out the path.

Another path near Lee Road connects The Baths to Spring Bay.

Virgin Gorda

Other Beaches

The Baths and the beaches within Devil's Bay Park are the most popular beach areas on Virgin Gorda, but they are by no means the only ones. Some others follow (from south to north)

Savannah Bay & Pond Bay

Just north of Spanish Town you'll see a rocky road that leads to two of the island's best beaches. While you can drive to Savannah Beach, Pond Beach is accessible only on foot, or from the sea. Undeveloped, but prime real estate for new villas, these are the best shelling beaches on the island. You'll find cowries, helmuts, sand dollars and sea biscuits all along the shore. Snorkeling is good here as well, and Savannah has a marked underwater trail. Look for the access road off North Shore Road.

Nail Bay & Mahoe Bay

Farther north along the western coast, these bays both front resorts. **Nail Bay Resort** and **Mango Bay Resort** allow non-guests to rent watersports equipment. They also have places for light dining.

Leverick Bay

The **Leverick Bay Resort** has a small beach with the busiest watersports rental shack on Virgin Gorda. They also have a beachside eatery.

Bercher's Bay & Deep Bay

These beaches are on the peninsula that juts into North Sound. They are accessible from both Biras Creek and the Bitter End Yacht Club.

Vixen Point Beach on Prickly Pear Island and **Hay Point Beach** on Mosquito Island (both in North Sound) are accessible only by boat. They are secluded and have calm waters for swimming. There are beach shacks for light dining.

Watersports

The resort hotels have active watersports centers. Guests at these hotels have free use of snorkel gear, Sunfish, windsurf boards and kayaks. The island's best-known scuba diving operators have offices at the hotels as well. You can arrange scuba and snorkel trips through the hotel concierge, but if you are in a villa community or an in-town hotel, you can easily make arrangements on your own.

Scuba Diving

Dive BVI, which has offices at the Virgin Gorda Yacht Harbour, ☎ (284) 495-5513, and at Leverick Bay, ☎ (284) 495-7328, is the largest dive operator on the island. They work with virtually every hotel on Virgin Gorda. Dives are organized daily to nearby dive sites as Cockroach Island, West Dog and Great Dog. The most popular trip is to The Wreck of the *Rhone* (see page 44, 156) off Salt Island. Dive BVI offers introductory scuba lessons, PADI certification courses and such special courses as night diver, underwater photographer and underwater naturalist. They pick up at hotel docks or meet you on your boat. Write Box 1040, Virgin Gorda, BVI, or check their website at www.divebvi.com.

Burt Kilbride's Sunchaser Scuba is based at the Bitter End Yacht Club on North Sound, ☎ (284) 495-9638). Kilbride's is renowned in the BVI and was one of the first operators in the area. They conduct two dives each day to destinations such as Ginger Island, the Dog Islands and the Wreck of the *Rhone* (dive sites vary every day). They offer resort courses as well as full certification courses. Write Burt Kilbride, Box 46, Virgin Gorda or check the website at www.sunchaserscuba.com.

Day-Sails & Snorkeling

Bring a hat, towel and sunscreen.

Day-sail ships head to nearby islands, primarily uninhabited, for snorkeling, but they also sail to Anegada and Peter Island. Full-day trips include lunch. Full- or half-day trips include an open bar and all snorkel gear.

Euphoric Cruises at the Virgin Gorda Yacht Harbour, ☎ (284) 495-5542, or www.bviboats.com, **Spice Charters** at Leverick Bay, ☎ (284) 496-6633. www.spicebvi.com, and the *Spirit of Anegada*, ☎ (284) 495-5937, www.spiritofanegada.com, are three good choices. They all offer sailing trips, snorkeling and island hopping.

Learn to Sail or Windsurf

The **Bitter End Yacht Club** sponsors a sailing school that caters to all levels of ability. They also offer lessons to those who want to improve their windsurfing skills (known as boardsailing in the BVI). You need not be a hotel guest to take lessons. Write Bitter End Sailing School, Box 46, Virgin Gorda, ☎ (284) 494-2745 or see www.beyc.com.

Deep-Sea Fishing

Fishing is both a livelihood and a sport here. There are hard-fought competitions year-round. Contestants come from all over the world. **Island Boyz** offers one-day or one-week fishing trips, ☎ (284) 495-6168, islandboyz@surfbvi.com. Another good choice, **Walford Farrington**, has his 24-foot speedboat docked at Leverick Bay. He organizes both full- and half-day trips. ☎ (284) 495-7612.

Glass-Bottomed Boat

Explore the clear waters of the BVI without getting wet. Contact **North Sound Water Sports** for schedules, ☎ (284) 495-7558, www.bviwatersports.com.

Watersports Gear Rentals

The best place to rent watersports gear is at Leverick Bay. They offer powerboat and dinghy rentals. They also rent Hobie Wave sailboats, Sunfish, snorkel gear and sea kayaks. You can arrange parasailing and water skiing through **Leverick Bay Watersports**, ☎ (284) 495-7376, watersports@ surfbvi.com.

Double D Charters is your best bet if you'd like to rent a sailboat or powerboat for a day of sightseeing and snorkeling at islands south of Virgin Gorda. Their offices are at the Virgin Island Yacht Harbour, ☎ (284) 495-6150, www.doubledbvi.com.

Land-Based Activities

Tennis

There are tennis courts at **Biras Creek Resort**, ☎ (284) 494-3555, **Leverick Bay Resort**, ☎ (284) 495-7421, and **Nail Bay Resort**, ☎ (284) 494-8000. **Little Dix Bay Resort** has seven courts. They are managed by Peter Burwash International and have a lovely setting amid colorful trees and plants. The pro shop sells balls and lessons are given. Guests get preference, but you can reserve a court for a fee. ☎ (284) 495-5555.

Horseback Riding

Alex Parillon is based near Savannah Bay and many of his rides begin or end there. ☎ (284) 499-3984.

Hiking

Gorda Peak National Park

At 1,360 feet, Gorda Peak is the highest point on Virgin Gorda. It stands amid 265 acres of Caribbean Dry Forest. The land was donated to the National Parks Trust by conservationist Lawrence Rockefeller in 1974 and was designated as a nature preserve. Since the island gets only 30 inches of rainfall annually, the vegetation grows low to the ground and you'll see lots of cactus, tamarinds and frangipanis. These have adapted to the dry conditions, as have other plants, which have waxy leaves that prevent water evaporation.

Be alert for a bushy plant with red seeds that have black eyes. These are called crab eyes and are poisonous.

Three miles out of Spanish Town, you'll reach a trail leading to Gorda Park (there are two others, but parking is best here). The trails are easy to negotiate and the trek should take 30 minutes or so. En route you'll see a variety of plants and herbs, including bay trees (bay leaves are used in making cologne), black wattle (used to brew medicinal tea), and poison ash.

Lizards of all kinds slither through the underbrush, butterflies and birds fly overhead, and hermit crabs and racer snakes (I was assured they are harmless) rest beside the rocks.

> **Did you know?** There are three species of tree frogs here. The most common is the Virgin Islands "Bo-Peep," which gets its name from the sound it makes.

The park is home to the world's smallest reptile, the Virgin Gorda gecko.

From the Observation Tower you have a great view of many islands and cays, as the Sir Francis Drake Channel spreads before you. Tortola is the largest land mass and beyond it you'll see Jost Van Dyke. The tiny island nearby is Fallen Jerusalem (look for the rock pile), then there are Ginger, Cooper, Salt and Pepper islands. If the day is very clear you might catch a glimpse of Anegada to the northeast. Virgin Gorda's North Sound and the cays near it look almost close enough to touch.

North Sound Trail (Nail Bay Ruins)

If you enjoy hiking, try the North Sound Trail, which runs along the west side of Gorda Mountain (follow North Sound Road to Pond Bay, turn left at the fork and park near the restroom). As you climb, you have a great view of St. John and, in the distance, St. Thomas. Soon you'll pass four little houses – bear right and you'll find yourself at Nail Bay Ruins. You can easily find the ruins. A sugar cane plantation once stood on this site. The stone structure was probably the overseer's cottage. There's the factory with boiling bench and, nearby, the stone horsemill where the cane was crushed. The slave village was probably below the factory on the slope, its houses constructed of wattle wood with earthen floors and palm leaf thatch roofs. If you head back along the trail, you'll reach Nail Bay (beyond your car), where you can snorkel, go shelling and admire graceful blue herons and spotted sandpipers.

Virgin Gorda

North Sound Walks

Remember to wear a hat, use sunscreen and bring water. It can get very hot.

Several well-maintained walking trails start from **Biras Creek**. One climbs from the road that connects the resort and Deep Bay and circles around **Biras Hill**. Several kinds of cactus and orchids grow in the area. From Bercher's Beach you can follow the trail to **Bercher's Bluff**. It passes through stunted vegetation that is neatly trimmed by the prevailing winds from the sea. The summit of the trail provides an excellent view that contrasts the rolling waves of the bay with the peaceful calm of the sound.

Mosquito Island

Mosquito Island has shoreline trails that lead from Drake's Anchorage (the resort here is closed) to **Book Rock** on the west and to beautiful **Honeymoon Bay** on the east. To reach the island's highest point (252 feet), look for the path from Honeymoon Beach. From the peak you can see the Sound.

Spas

The Spa at Little Dix Bay

The spa is built on a commanding bluff above the resort's villas. It opened for the 2003 winter season and has been well received. The two-tiered infinity pool is where guests relax before their treatments. The hub of the spa is an open-air pavilion that is linked to individual treatment cottages by stone paths. There are 10 therapists. Services include scrubs, wraps and massages. The stone massage is very popular. There are several types of facials, including one that offers sun relief. Therapies for hands and feet and reflexology are aloso available, along with manicures and pedicures. The spa offers group and private yoga classes. It is open from 8 am to 8 pm daily and advance reservations are a must. ☎ (284) 495-5555, www.littledixbay.com.

The Spa at Leverick Bay

While not as luxurious as Little Dix Bay's spa, the services offered are comparable. Therapists here offer both Swedish and Indian-style massages, acupuncture, seaweed and sea salt wraps, facials and reflexology. Additionally, they offer "sugaring" (hair removal), manicures, pedicures and hair braiding. Rates are less expensive than those at Little Dix Bay. You need to reserve in advance. ☎ (284) 495-7375, www.savezoneinc.net/salon.

The Best Shops

Virgin Gorda Yacht Harbour

 There are boutiques in the resort hotels but the island's primary shopping center is adjacent to Virgin Gorda Yacht Harbour. While there are only a dozen shops, they are an eclectic mix selling resort wear, island T-shirts and souvenirs, local art and crafts, as well as music. They are individually owned and do not all keep the same business hours. Generally, they are open from 9 am to 1 pm and 2 to 5 pm, Monday through Saturday, and 10 am to 2 pm on Sunday. They accept credit cards.

The Blue Banana, the **Nauti-Virgin**, **Dive BVI**, **Next Wave** and the **BVI Apparel Outlet** all sell tropical clothing, bathing suits, cover-ups and pareos, T-shirts, hats, gift items, sunglasses and beach bags.

Thee Artistic Gallery sells prints, colorful wall hangings, antique maps of the BVI, pottery, crystal and collectible coins.

Virgin Gorda

The Virgin Gorda Craft Shop features works by nature artisans, including Coppermine design clothing and fabrics.

The Wine Cellar and Bakery has a wide selection of wines, spirits, cheeses and breads.

Kaunda's sells CDs, DVDs and cameras. Reggae, calypso and steel pans are featured.

Ocean Delight offers ice cream, while **Island Drug Centre** has cosmetics and over-the-counter medicines.

Buck's Market sells grocery items, fresh fruits and vegetables, meats and fish. Open 7 am to 8 pm, Monday through Saturday, and 7 am to 7 pm on Sunday.

Leverick Bay Resort

A smaller selection of good boutiques can be found at the Leverick Bay Resort. They include a **Pusser's Company Store** that sells its trademark items, including rum in gift packaging, its own brand of sportswear, hats and travel bags. **The Palm Tree Gallery** has colorful attractive gift items including serving trays, wall hangings and paintings. There's a good selection of handcrafted jewelry. **The Chef's Pantry** is a mini-market offering deli, sandwiches and provisions for those on charters.

Bitter End Yacht Club

The Emporium at Bitter End Yacht Club is a gourmet food shop, mostly take-out, and **The Reeftique** next door sells island crafts, jewelry, gifts and sportswear.

Biras Creek

Fat Virgin's Treasure, part of Biras Creek's beachfront eatery, sells gift items and island sportswear.

Best Places to Stay

While the high season accommodation crunch has been relieved a bit by the addition of several villa communities, Virgin Gorda still does not have a large number of places to stay. What is also clear is that it has virtually no inexpensive places.

The island is home to a select group of resort hotels. Facing a crescent beach, on a peninsula jutting into North Sound and a hillside overlooking the sea, these hotels are elegant without being flashy. Each offers a unique experience and has clearly been successful since guests seem to return year after year. These have been joined by a handful of villa communities on some of the island's loveliest bays.

There are a few small hotels in Spanish Town and there are privately owned villas for rental scattered around the island. Since amenities vary greatly at the villa communities, make sure to inquire about those that are important to you when making reservations. Explore special package rates offered by the hotels. Honeymoon packages are very popular.

Rates at the deluxe resorts often include meals (American Plan), or at least breakfast and dinner (Modified American Plan), along with unrestricted use of watersports gear. Though rates are high, you'll have virtually no other costs while on the island. A 7% government tax and a 10% daily service charge are added to each bill. Hotels accept major credit cards.

The Alive Scale

The scale is based on a double room in high season (December 15-April 15). Rates can be 25% less off-season, when package tours are also available.

Deluxe . . . . over $400
Expensive . . . . $300-$400
Moderate . . . . $200-$299

Resorts

Little Dix Bay
Box 70 Virgin Gorda BVI
☎ (284) 495-5555, (800) 928-3000
www.littledixbay.com
Deluxe

When I first visited Little Dix Bay a number of years ago, there was a photo of a young Mohammed Ali on the lobby wall. His quote, "Hey man, this is paradise"!

Ninety-seven guest rooms (including four one-bedroom suites and two villas) follow the curve of a long crescent beach. They blend into the landscape so completely that those arriving by boat do not see any buildings. They are cleverly tucked behind a grove of seagrape trees and coconut palms. The grounds (500 acres) are extraordinary, dotted with towering saman, mahogany and white cedar trees that have tiny white flowers. A veritable army of gardeners tends the grounds.

White cedar trees produce the national flower of the BVI.

Little Dix Bay was conceived by Laurence Rockefeller and managed by Rockresorts until 1993 when Rosewood Hotels assumed ownership. They set out to revitalize paradise and in many subtle but substantial ways they have done so. Accommodations vary from oceanfront rooms with patios and terraces to the original hexagonal cottages set in pairs behind the beach. Some of these are on stilts. The suites are also arranged in pairs, while the villas are set apart, near the spa. They have two or three bedrooms and full kitchens, as well as private pools.

Rooms have been redecorated using lighter woods, bamboos and wickers, pastel shades and tropical fabrics. They are casual yet elegant with accent pieces from the Pacific Rim. Rooms are air-conditioned but ceiling fans remain and are sufficient for all but a few nights. Bathrooms too have been redone to add better lighting and fixtures.

There is no pressure to do anything. Lounge chairs, water floats, Sunfish and kayaks are placed along the beach each morning. Snorkel gear must be signed out at the Beach House and you can join the free snorkel trips to nearby reefs, snorkel in the bay or hop a cab and snorkel at The Baths, nearby (see pages 119-20). You can arrange to water-ski at nearby Pond Bay too. The hotel has a flotilla of Boston Whalers and a crewmember will whisk you to Spring Bay or Savannah Bay (picnic lunch is packed for you) and return at your request. Scuba trips (with Dive BVI) and deep-sea fishing are available at additional cost.

There are seven tennis courts (two can be lit at night) and a full pro shop. Two easy-to-follow trails are on property and a handful of jogging paths. Walking through the grounds, you'll notice that the landscape is not highly manicured but rather seems to be a natural flow of flowers and foliage. This is in keeping with Rockefeller's intention of fostering an eco-friendly island environment.

Virgin Gorda

There are two first-rate amenities for guest use. The fitness center has treadmills, lifecycles, Cybex weight machines and free weights. A personal trainer offers group aerobic, stretching and toning classes as well as private sessions. The spa has 10 individual treatment rooms for massages, facials and scrubs. (Read more about the spa on page 128.)

Ages three and up are catered for here, and there are special activities for teens.

Rosewood has done more than renovate and add amenities. They have changed Little Dix Bay's philosophy so guests are younger, more active and child-friendly. There's a Children's Grove (near the Beach House), where exuberant instructors play calypso music, tell tall tales about pirates and set out materials for arts and crafts.

There are three restaurants at Little Dix Bay. The Pavilion, four intertwined Polynesian pyramids that face the sea, serves buffet breakfasts and lunches. Candlelit dinners are more formal with a continental menu. The Sugar Mill is open air and serves dinner and Sunday brunch. The menu is West Indian. The Beach House Grill is adjacent to the resort dock and only a few steps from the beach. Light lunches are served here and at night fresh grilled seafood including Anegada lobster and steaks are menu highlights. Tiki torches tucked into the sand create a romantic glow. (More on the restaurants in *Hotel Dining*).

The final ingredient is the most important, for it makes all the others work. The staff, most of whom have worked here for many years, is exceptional. Warm, friendly and helpful, they make you feel at home.

If this isn't paradise, it's close.

Note: On a bluff above the resort, Little Dix Bay is building private villas. One section has been completed and is virtually sold out

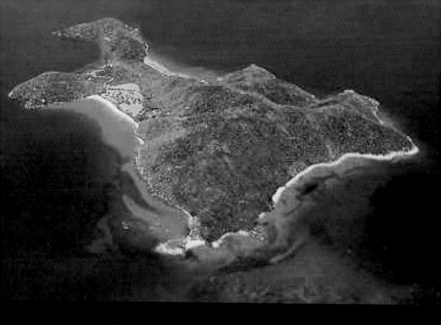

Above: Guana Island (www.guana.com)

Below: Guana Bay from the hills (www.garages.org/guanabaybeach.html)

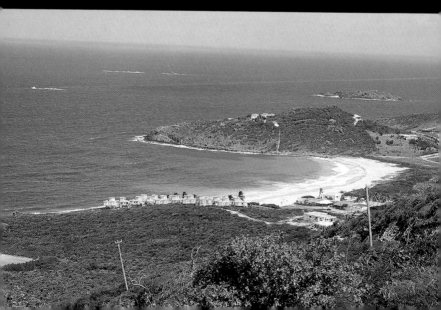

Above: Deadman's Bay, Peter Island (www.miroworld.com)

Below: Peter Island beach (www.britishvirginislands.de)

*Above: Looking down on Deadman's Bay, Peter Island
(www.peterislandmedia.com)*

Below: Saba Island

while the other section is under construction. Some may be available for rental. Guests (and owners) have full use of hotel facilities.

On North Sound

At the edge of Virgin Gorda, a lagoon called North Sound is formed, protected by natural breakfronts of live coral reefs and beach-fringed cays. For centuries the peninsula extending into the lagoon was called the "Bitter End." This was the turn-back point for sailors – the last point of land before the open waters of the Atlantic. This peninsula, which is accessible only by boat, houses two unique stops, The Bitter End Yacht Club and Biras Creek Resort. On the mainland, overlooking North Sound, stands Leverick Bay Resort, which is accessible by road as well.

Getting to these places is half the fun. If you fly into Virgin Gorda or arrive on a ferry from Tortola or St. Thomas, your hotel will arrange for a car to meet and drive you across the island to Gun Creek. The Bitter End and Biras Creek ferries will carry you across the Sound. An option for those flying into Beef Island/Tortola airport is the North Sound Express, which makes several crossings daily from the dock at Trellis Bay (Beef Island) to The Bitter End. The ride takes 30 minutes. A Biras Creek water taxi will meet this ferry. Arrange this transportation when making your hotel reservations.

Biras Creek Resort
North Sound
Box 54, Virgin Gorda
☎ (284) 494-3555, (800) 223-1108
www.biras.com
Deluxe

As the water taxi approaches Biras Creek, your eyes will be drawn to the circular stone building on a hill-

Virgin Gorda

The hotel is a member of the prestigious Relais et Châteaux group.

top at center stage. Looking like a Crusader castle, this peak-roofed building houses the resort's open-sided restaurant. Food here is considered exceptional, as is the restaurant's wine list.

A small resort, Biras Creek sits on a strip of land between two hills on a peninsula. It is touched by three distinct bodies of water: North Sound Lagoon, the Atlantic Ocean and the Caribbean Sea. These allow a broad watersports program to flourish.

The hotel's 60 guests are housed in 31 suites. Twenty oceanside suites stand along Bercher's Bay on the Atlantic, while eight other suites are in a landscaped garden. They are identical in size and layout, each having an air-conditioned bedroom, a good-size comfortably furnished sitting area with wicker and rattan chairs and tables, along with a private verandah. The refrigerator is stocked with welcome beverages and there's a tea- and coffeemaker. A really nice touch is the outdoor shower enclosed by tall walls and colorful plants to protect your privacy. Each suite has two bicycles, which are the most common mode of transport at Biras Creek.

The two Grand Suites face the sea. They also have one bedroom and even more amenities, such as free-standing bathtubs and open-air toilets, bidets and showers.

The Premier Suite has two bedrooms and two baths. Each bedroom has an open-air verandah and there is a closed one between them.

The hotel's 140 acres are criss-crossed by marked nature trails, stonewalled gardens and a mangrove pond with unusual birds and wildlife. The freshwater swimming pool sits at beachside. Lunch is served here several days a week. The private beach, named Deep Bay, can be reached on foot or by bicycle. The active watersports program is based here too. Guests have the use of a wide variety of non-motor-ized water toys. Among them are Hobie Cats, Sun-fish and Laser sailboats, windsurf boards and sea kayaks. The staff gives lessons as well. Guided snor-keling trips are led several days a week and a fleet of Boston Whalers is available should guests want to explore North Sound.

The spa has two suites and offers body and facial treatments. Massages are offered in the spa, guest rooms and terraces and in the massage hut on the beach. Outdoor yoga classes are given.

There are two lighted tennis courts. After dinner, guests gather in the library/den, where there is a snooker table and large-screen TV.

Biras Creek has a marina and yachts also anchor offshore and come for dinner at the Fat Virgin Café nearby. There is a boutique here as well.

The Bitter End Yacht Club & Resort
North Sound
Box 46, Virgin Gorda BVI
☎ (284) 494-2745, (800) 872-2392
www.beyc.com
Expensive

The Bitter End, which was born as a family retreat, has grown into a destination resort that most cap-tures the water-based culture of the BVI. Guests at this luxurious yet casual stop can choose on-land ac-commodations in beachfront villas or hillside suites, or they can stay aboard a yacht and still enjoy the hotel's amenities. Provisioning the yacht is part of the rate. Many opt for a combination of the two. The Bitter End is also home to a full-service marina with 70 moorings and a gourmet provision shop. Here too you'll find The Bitter End sailing and windsurfing school, Kilbrides Sunchaser Scuba and a first-rate watersports program.

There are 85 guest rooms. Beachfront villas resemble West Indian cottages, with sea views and hammocks. They have wraparound verandahs. The suites are on the hillside facing North Sound. They have separate bedrooms and comfortable sitting areas. Furnishings emphasize light wickers, rattans and colorful cotton fabrics. All accommodations have many amenities. The Freedom 30 yachts can sleep six. They can day-sail and return to the resort each night for dinner or can anchor at dive sites around the islands.

Obviously, most guests are watersports enthusiasts or sailors.

Hotel facilities include a private beach and swimming pool. The watersports center has over 100 boats for guest use and they offer excursions around North Sound almost daily. They also have sailboards, snorkel gear and kayaks. They offer lessons. There are three restaurants at The Bitter End (See *Best Places to Eat*, page 153).

Leverick Bay Resort and Marina

Box 63, Virgin Gorda
☎ (284) 495-7421
www.leverickbay.com
Moderate

With one of the island's most beautiful settings, Leverick Bay Resort is crowded most of the year. It is the only North Sound resort that can be reached by car because it is on the Sound's southern shore and not on the peninsula.

One of the liveliest stops on Virgin Gorda, it has the largest supply of watersports gear for rental (see page 125) and an active marina. An office of Dive BVI (see page 123) is also located here.

The resort is small, with only 14 guest rooms and four guest suites. The accommodations are located above the pool and sea in a string of bi-level buildings with pastel peaked roofs. The rooms are comfortably furnished with rattan, tropical fabrics and two double beds. There is an unstocked refrigerator, cable TV and private balcony. The one- and two-bedroom suites – Ginger, Nutmeg, Spice and Cinnamon – are a bit more luxurious. The bedrooms are air-conditioned and there are kitchen facilities. There is a double-size sleeping sofa. The wrap-around terraces face North Sound and Mosquito Island; they have grills.

The resort has a beautiful whale-shaped pool and sundeck, but most guests head to the beach where water toys and boats can be signed out. There is a beach bar and restaurant. The resort's main restaurant (see *Dining*, page 153) is near the pool. The shops include a Pusser's Company Store, Palm Tree Gallery for crafts and gifts and The Chef's Pantry, for gourmet take-out. Leverick Bay's Spa is open to non-guests. Reservations are essential.

Spanish Town

Fischer's Cove Beach Hotel
Box 60, The Valley
Virgin Gorda, BVI
☎ (284) 495-5252
www.fischerscove.com
Inexpensive

A traditional West Indian Hotel, Fischer's Cove is on the island's southwestern coast. You can walk into Spanish Town from here and the hotel has its own beach. There are eight freestanding cottages for rent – six are one-bedroom studios, while the other two have two bedrooms. Triangular in shape and comfortably, if basically, furnished, they have private showers, ceiling fans and kitchenettes with microwaves and coffeemakers. Daily maid service is included.

There are 12 guest rooms in the bi-level main house. The garden-view rooms are air-conditioned and have cable TV. The ocean-view rooms have ceiling fans. The hotel's restaurant is set on a seaside patio. It is best known for its West Indian food and lobster dinners.

Ocean View Hotel
Box 66, Lee Road
The Valley, Virgin Gorda
☎ (284) 495-5230
Inexpensive

Directly opposite the Virgin Gorda Yacht Harbour, Ocean View, also known as The Wheel House for its West Indian restaurant, is a small locally owned hotel that looks like a large private house. Its 12 guest rooms are air-conditioned and have cable TV, but not all have private baths. This is a basic but acceptable choice for those who are not in their rooms much and to whom creature comforts are of minimal importance.

Villa Communities

Nail Bay Villas & Village
Box 69
Virgin Gorda BVI
☎ (284) 494-8000, (800) 871-3551
www.nailbay.com
Moderate-Expensive

On the site of a 19th-century sugar plantation, Nail Bay is one of Virgin Gorda's most intriguing stops. Nestled on a lush tropical hillside overlooking three of the island's most stunning beaches, Nail Bay is both a villa community and a resort, with suites, rooms and apartments for rent.

The villas are privately owned and were built to suit the individual owners' architectural preferences. Some are quite luxurious, while others have West Indian charm. The furnishings also reflect the individual owner's taste, but all have fully equipped gourmet kitchens, washer/dryers, dishwashers and microwaves. Some have private pools and are air-conditioned.

Villas range in size from one bedroom to five bedrooms. Some face the beach, while others are scattered on the hillside.

Nail Bay's resort complex, **Island Time Village**, is set on a hillside overlooking the swimming pool and tennis court. The pastel-painted bi-level buildings house deluxe rooms, suites and apartments. The rooms have kitchenettes and a bathroom big enough to hold a Jacuzzi for two. They offer views of the sea from their private terrace. The suites have a separate bedroom as well as a living room and full kitchen. Two wall beds in the living room are great for children, but families might prefer the apartments, which have from one to three bedrooms. They are quite luxurious, with central air conditioning, indoor and outdoor dining areas, large decks and Jacuzzis.

The spacious grounds are beautifully maintained and planted. The ruins of the sugar plantation have been restored and weddings and parties are often held there. There are two freshwater pools, a cooling waterfall, outdoor whirlpool, one tennis court that can be lit, a bocce court and croquet field.

Three beach strips are part of the resort and the snorkeling is first-rate, with a coral reef and caves to explore. The Dog and Dolphin Bar and Grill at poolside is a casual dining spot, but if you prefer to eat in, you can hire a talented local chef to prepare and serve your dinner.

Nail Bay is a 20-minute drive from Spanish Town. A car is a must.

Since the owners spend part of the year here as well, not every villa is available year-round.

Virgin Gorda

Mango Bay Resort

Box 1062, Virgin Gorda, BVI

☎ (284) 495-5672

www.mangobayresort.com

Moderate

The sparkling white resort villas at Mango Bay Resort were built in the late 1980s and there is room to expand along the hillside. On beautiful Mahoe Bay, about 15 minutes north of Spanish Town, the villas (from one to three bedrooms) can be rented for a day, week or month. Most stand on the beach shaded by palm trees and a few others are in a garden area nearby.

Designed for casual living and comfort, the ground-level suites have Italian and French furnishings with silk-covered sofas and marble tables. Each has a sleeper sofa in the living room and a fully equipped kitchen, including that great vacation aid, the dishwasher. There are kitchenette facilities on the deck so you can barbecue and eat outside.

You'll want to have a car here.

These suites (there are two in each villa) can be combined to form a three-bedroom apartment. Studio rooms on the upper level of some villas have white woods and kitchenettes. Daily maid service is a plus and for an additional fee management will provide a local cook.

Giorgio's Table is on Mahoe Bay's waterfront. Mahoe Bay is a beautiful secluded beach with a reef to snorkel and snorkel gear and kayaks are available for guest use.

Mango Bay Resort is the rental agency for two exclusive villas adjacent to it. See *Villa Rentals*, page 145.

Guavaberry Spring Bay Homes
Box 20
Virgin Gorda, BVI
☎ (284) 495-5227
www.guavaberryspringbay.com
Moderate
Guavaberry does not accept credit cards.

With a terrific location near Spring Bay Beach and
The Baths, this development has 18 rental homes.
They resemble tree houses, with louvered windows
and doors opening onto spacious terraces. They are
not identical, but generally speaking they are hexagonal wood-framed houses, neatly furnished with
white walls, tiled floors, colorful prints and lots of
green plants. There are one-bedroom or
two-bedroom units. All have fully furnished kitchens, a living room/dining area and furnished sun
decks. There is an on-site commissary. The grounds
are lovely, with colorful plants and the signature
boulders that mark this part of the island. There are
no resort amenities here, but Spring Bay Beach is a
stroll away and The Baths is also within walking
distance.

Olde Yard Village
Box 26, The Valley
Virgin Gorda, BVI
☎ (284) 495-5544
www.oldeyardvillage.com
Expensive

The island's newest condominium and townhouse
development is still under construction. On a
75-acre site at the edge of Spanish Town that for-
merly housed the Olde Yard Inn, this rising development is both residential and a resort. Encircled by a
privacy wall, its grounds are studded with stately
old trees as well as newly planted palm trees and
colorful gardens.

Virgin Gorda

The first 26 units are housed in three low-rise buildings. The apartments are good-size, with first-rate kitchen appliances and luxurious bathroom fixtures. The private terraces face the gardens or pool. Most have been sold. They will be individually decorated and some will be available for rental.

The second units are townhouses built on a hillside with views of the sea. There will be 10 units in five buildings. They range from studios to four-bedroom apartments and two-bedroom duplexes. These are slated for completion in 2006. as is an entertainment center. Amenities include an open-air Jacuzzi, swimming pool, two tennis courts, a squash court, a fitness center and a commissary.

La Brasserie Bistro, with the same ownership as Giorgio's Table restaurant, sits at poolside. Olde Yard Village is not near the water so you should consider a rental car. The owners here are very knowledgeable about Virgin Gorda and quite helpful.

Private Villa Rentals

There are privately owned villas scattered throughout Virgin Gorda. Many are represented by agencies.

Virgin Gorda Villa Rentals

This is the island's largest rental agency. Their villas are in Leverick Bay and Mahoe Bay. They often have a seven-night minimum stay policy. ☎ (284) 495-7421; www.virgingordabvi.com.

A Dream Come True Villa Rentals

They represent 40 luxurious villas and own one (see below). ☎ (978) 526-1329, www.bvidreamvilla.com.

Hunter Homes Ltd.

This is a smaller agency that represents a cluster of two- and three-bedroom homes on a hilltop overlooking the sea. Contact them at ☎ (315) 865-4475, www.hunterhomesbvi.com.

Private Villas at Mango Bay Resort

Mango Bay Resort is the rental and management agency for two spectacular villas that stand on a rocky outcrop a five-minute stroll away. Both are deluxe.

Katitche Point Greathouse, built by British architect, Michael Helm, and completed in early 2000, is a holiday retreat for a large family, group of friends or a small wedding party. The main house, in pyramid shape, has four large double-room suites, each with a private bath. These bedrooms open onto an inner courtyard with lemon trees and a flower garden. An even more spacious master bedroom suite has its own kitchenette and its terrace features an open-air shower and bath.

The main house has a state-of-the-art kitchen and a dining table that seats 14. The wrap-around terrace has a breakfast nook. There is a horizon pool that overlooks both Mahoe and Pond Bays. The second level has a library, wide screen TV, VCR and DVD players and a video collection.

Mango Bay Resort provides daily maid service and a gardener to care for the pool and grounds. They can hire a chef as well. The Greathouse can be rented only as a unit. For more details check www.kititchepoint.com.

Nearby, overlooking Savannah Bay, stands **A Dream Come True Villa**, with 6,000 square feet of accommodations in two separate buildings clustered around a horizon pool. The Caribe House is the main building. It has a spacious living room, a gourmet kitchen and dining area that can seat 12. There are two bedrooms in the Caribe House. Across the patio stands the Bali Pod, which also has two bedrooms. Sliding glass doors open to a roof-covered verandah. An outdoor bar and refrigerator is near the pool. Guests enjoy the use of two kayaks and all the amenities of the Mango Bay Resort. For more details check www.bvidreamvilla.com.

For rental information, contact The Mango Bay Resort, ☎ (284) 495-5672, mangobay@surfbvi.com.

Best Places to Dine

Virgin Gorda's dining options, which were once confined to hotel dining rooms and small basic stops serving Caribbean specialties, have expanded. While the resort hotels still have the most elegant eateries, a good number of attractive restaurants have opened in Spanish Town and in the new villa communities. Their menus are more varied as well. If you'd like to dine at one of the North Sound hotels, accessible only by boat, you can arrange transport when making your reservation.

The Alive Scale

The price scale is based on the cost of dinner (per person, three courses and coffee) without alcoholic beverages. To keep costs down, stick to local seafood dishes and the in-town choices.

Deluxe. . . . . over $50
Expensive . . . . $35-$50
Moderate . . . . under $35

Tip: Restaurants are quite small so it makes sense to reserve for dinner. All the restaurants that follow accept major credit cards.

Giorgio's Table
Mahoe Bay
☎ (284) 495-5684
Expensive

There is a jetty at Giorgio's Table for those arriving by boat.

Location, location, location, and the food is delicious as well. Perched at the water's edge on Pond Bay, you can hear the waves bounce off the open terrace where there are a few tables. The indoor dining room has tall glass windows so you can see the twinkling lights of Tortola in the distance. The menu features Mediterranean dishes combined with Caribbean seafood and fruits. You'll find tuna with mango and kiwi, lobster risotto, pumpkin ravioli and a score of pastas. Filet mignon with mushrooms, veal scallopini and porcini mushroom crêpes are other popular choices. Desserts include homemade kalhua tiramisu and strawberry sorbet. The lunch menu includes ravioli, lasagna and excellent pizza. Giorgio's has a fine wine cellar. Reserve for dinner. Casual chic at dinner. Informal at lunch.

Chez Bamboo
Spanish Town
☎ (284) 495-5239
Moderate

A two-minute walk from the Yacht Harbour (look for the aqua-colored fence) and under the same management as the Bath and Turtle Tavern, Chez Bamboo is an attractive bistro with candlelit tables and starched, colorful tablecloths. There are tables indoors as well as in the courtyard.

Starters include onion soup, lobster bisque with chunks of fresh lobster, and local fishcakes with aioli sauce. Chilled shrimp, lobster ceviche, fried calamari and pasta dishes are popular entrées. Prime

Virgin Gorda

rib is served Saturday nights. Chocolate pecan torte and mango cheesecake are delicious desserts.

There's live jazz in the courtyard Friday nights. The "martini" bar opens at 5 pm. Chez Bamboo is often crowded with diners from yachts anchored in the harbor. Dinner only. Casual chic.

La Brasserie
Olde Yarde Village
Spanish Town
☎ (284) 495-6994
Moderate-Expensive

Part of a new villa community that is springing up at the site of the former Olde Yarde Inn on the edge of Spanish Town, La Brasserie is managed by Giorgio's Table (see above). The Brasserie sits at poolside in a beautiful garden among palm and other tropical trees. Lunch, served from 12-3, offers a daily soup, salads, pastas and quiches. Dinner includes an antipasti selection, tuna tartare, pizza, grilled lobster, steak and local fish. It's early dining here – the kitchen closes at 8:30 pm. There may be construction noise at lunch. Informal.

Bath and Turtle Tavern
Yacht Harbour
☎ (284) 495-5239
Inexpensive-Moderate

Live music Wednesday nights. Informal.

No reservations are required at this casual tavern in the Yacht Harbour shopping arcade. It serves all three meals, opening at 7:30 am for breakfast. The kitchen closes at 10 pm, but the bar stays open later. There are tables on the covered patio and indoors as well. The lunch menu leans toward burgers, salads and sandwiches, as well as a variety of pizzas. The dinner menu features barbecue ribs, Anegada fish fingers, tamarind ginger chicken wings, fried chicken and jerk chicken wraps. Dinner salads include seared ahi tuna and chicken Caesar. There are daily specials. Sunday brunch is always crowded.

Top of the Baths
The Valley
☎ (284) 495-5497
Inexpensive-Moderate

Situated at the entrance to The Baths and with stunning views of Tortola and the Sir Francis Drake Channel, this dining spot is bustling from its 8 am opening till it closes its doors after dinner. It has expanded and now has indoor dining as well as open-air tables. The lunch menu offers burgers, soups, salads and sandwiches as well as some typical Caribbean favorites. The dinner menu is heartier, with Cornish hens, steaks, local lobsters and grilled local fish. Pecan pie and chocolate cheesecake are popular desserts. Top of the Baths is part of a mini-mall with shops selling souvenirs and gifts. Informal.

MAD DOG

A tiny spot at the entrance to The Baths, this is a popular watering hole. It serves drinks and sandwiches from 10 am-7 pm. Informal. ☎ (284) 495-5380.

The Rock Café
Tower Road, Spanish Town
☎ (284) 495-5482
Moderate

You can walk from Spanish Town along Tower Road to The Rock Café (15 minutes), but the restaurant offers shuttle service from your accommodation as well. The liveliest dining spot here, The Rock has a beautiful location and Virgin Gorda's famed boulders. There is an air-conditioned dining room as well

Virgin Gorda

as an open-air patio. Tables on the patio are um-
brella-covered. There are many Italian dishes on the
menu, including bruschetta, spaghetti with lobster,
penne caprese and chicken piccata. A personal favorite is swordfish Sicilian-style. There are also
huge burgers, chicken wings and chicken or shrimp
Caesar salads. Pizzas too. There is live music at
night. The tequila bar stays open late.

Flying Iguana
Virgin Gorda Airport
☎ (284) 495-5277
Moderate

Located at the tiny airport and looking out to the
sea, Flying Iguana's dining room is decorated with
local artwork. Owned by one of the island's foremost
caterers, this small dining spot has an unusually
large and varied menu. Breakfast is served daily,
but the Sunday menu includes a half-dozen eggs
Benedict specials, as well as a lobster omelet. Breakfast is served till 3 pm. The full-day menu starts at
10 am. It includes fritters of conch, lobster, shellfish
and codfish. Caesar salads with grilled chicken or
bay shrimp or lobster are light main courses. Burgers, rack of lamb, coconut curry shrimp, blackened
steak, chicken or fish are served with vegetables and
potatoes. Informal.

Mine Shaft Café
Coppermine Point
☎ (284) 495-5260
Moderate

Young islanders head here for the gorgeous sunsets
and the free-flowing drinks at Happy Hour. A casual
spot, its menu is filled with barbecue ribs, burgers,
salads and chicken breast sandwiches. There's a
mini-golf course here too.

West Indian Restaurants

Two small basic spots specialize in traditional West
Indian specialties. Homey and family-run, they
serve curries, conch, local fish and soups. The nicer
of the two, **The Crab Hole in the Valley**, ☎ (284)
495-5307, serves from 11:30 am to midnight. **Anything Goes**, on Airport Road, no phone, serves from
10 am till 10 pm. Neither accepts credit cards.

Hotel Dining

Virgin Gorda's resort hotels offer guests and visitors
a variety of dining choices ranging from casual
beachfront eateries to elegant dining rooms serving
gourmet cuisine and fine wines.

Little Dix Bay
The Valley
☎ (284) 495-5555
Deluxe

Three distinct dining options are offered at Little
Dix Bay. The main dining room, **The Pavilion**, is an
open patio covered by a distinctive Polynesian-style
roof. All the tables have a view of the sea. Opulent
buffets are served for both breakfast and lunch. Dinner features American cuisine with delicious Caribbean and Pacific touches served by candlelight.
There's live music each evening. One recent menu
started with carpaccio of beef filet and lobster with
mustard dressing and Italian-style bean soup. They
were followed by seafood risotto, rack of lamb, several pastas and steak au poivre. Dinner dress code
means men need collared shirts and trousers, while
casual chic is required for women.

The adjacent **Sugar Mill Restaurant** serves dinner only and is closed Sunday and Monday. It's an
open-air eatery so you can dine under star-filled

Virgin Gorda

*Reservations
for dinner
are required
at The Pa-
vilion and
Sugar Mill.*

The Beach House Grill is less expensive than the other two choices.

skies. The kitchen is open, so you can watch chefs grill seafood and meats to your taste. A contemporary Caribbean menu is served here and occasionally there's a West Indian buffet. Informal attire.

Even more casual fare is served at **The Beach House Grill**, which is on the beach. The lunch menu has sandwiches and salads but the dinner menu features grilled meats, fresh seafood and innovative appetizers. Informal attire.

Biras Creek
North Sound
☎ (284) 494-3555 VHF #16
Deluxe-Expensive

The restaurant at Biras Creek is set in a stone castle atop a hill overlooking the resort. The menu features light foods and lots of fresh fruits and vegetables. Lunch is served here several days a week, but on other days it is served beachside. The buffet has salads, cheeses, grilled meats and fish. There is a prix fixe four-course dinner each night, as well as an à la carte menu. One dinner started with a lobster cake and stir fry vegetables or a salad with artichokes, green beans and mushrooms. The house specialty is a fresh half-lobster grilled, and there are meat dishes as well. There is a cheese table for dessert. The wine list here is excellent. Dress code at dinner means no shorts. Reservations are a must. A water taxi will meet you at Gun Creek Jetty.

Fat Virgin's Café, open daily from 10 am-9 pm. Informal. ☎ (284) 495-7052. At the marina dock near Biras Creek, it is a casual spot serving breakfast, lunch and dinner. The menu offers burgers, sandwiches, homemade soups and frozen drinks.

Lighthouse Restaurant
Leverick Bay Hotel
North Sound
☎ (284) 495-7154
Moderate-Expensive

For a while this delightful restaurant at Leverick Bay Hotel was managed by Pusser's and it remains akin to their restaurant at Soper's Hole, Tortola. A bi-level restaurant, it serves lunch and dinner on an open patio and dinner at a more formal second-floor dining room. This area has a popular bar and couches with comfortable pillows. Lunch includes British-style fish n' chips (served with vinegar), as well as sandwiches, burgers, conch fritters and pizza. The dinner menu includes peel-and-eat shrimp, fresh chowder and nachos. Entrées such as rack of lamb, fresh lobster and local fish and pastas are served upstairs with a great view of North Sound. There's live music several nights a week. Casual chic upstairs; informal on the patio.

Breakfast and light fare are served all day at the Beach Bar. The Chef's Pantry, a gourmet provision shop, is on the hillside.

Virgin Gorda

The Bitter End Yacht Club
North Sound
☎ (284) 494-2746. VHF #16
Expensive

Very popular with yachtsmen because of its launch service, The Bitter End serves cocktails and meals on a waterfront terrace overlooking North Sound. **The Clubhouse Steak and Seafood Grille** offers all three meals. The bar at the core of the restaurant was built from the wreck of a yacht and its mainmast is the centerpiece of the Grille. Breakfast and lunch are served buffet-style. Lunch has lots of salads, lobster cakes, cold cuts and cheeses. Dinner is served buffet-style or à la carte. The dinner menu has homemade soups, breads and desserts. Main courses include freshly caught fish and lobster, as well as steaks and pastas.

The English Carvery is not in the resort's main building, but is instead near the beach. It serves

A ferry will meet you at Gun Creek Jetty.

Reservations are a must at the Grille and Carvery. only dinner and special event nights are held here. Salads are served at tableside and the menu often has rack of lamb, curried shrimp and baked ham plus lots of vegetables. They, too, are served buffet-style. Dress is casual in both restaurants, but no shorts or T-shirts at dinner.

The English Pub is the most casual of the three dining choices in both fare and ambience. You can snack all day on homemade pizza, West Indian rotis, Cuban sandwiches and salads. The Pub is in The Emporium, a gourmet provision shop. Casual attire here.

After Dark

Virgin Gorda is the place to catch up on some zzzz's. There isn't much in the way of nightlife and what does exist is pretty tame. By midnight, the island is pretty well tucked in. Guests at Little Dix Bay, Biras Creek, The Bitter End and Leverick Bay Resort have live music during and after dinner most nights. There are faze bands (local pickup groups specializing in Caribbean and Latin music, steel pans and calypso or reggae under the stars. Spanish Town options include The Rock Café, where local gather to shoot the breeze and drink a cold brew. Upstairs, **Sam's Piano Bar** has a local pianist each night starting at 8 pm.

Chez Bamboo and **The Bath and Turtle**, sister restaurants in and near the Yacht Harbour have live music on different nights each week. It's often jazz. Check schedules in *Limin' Times*, the free entertainment guide.

The Mine Shaft Café on Coppermine Road has live music several nights a week and a Full-Moon Party monthly.

There is usually a live band or pianist at **Fischer's Cove Hotel**. Good reggae here.

If you are a night person, bring a deck of cards, some good books and a Walkman.

The Smaller Islands

Peter Island

Peter Island, the largest private island in the BVI, lies four miles southeast of Tortola in the Sir Francis Drake Channel. The **Peter Island Resort** owns virtually every acre of the 1,200 that comprise this fifth-largest island in the BVI chain. It's a resort that is always noted among the Caribbean's finest, and it is impressive. There is a young active crowd there and, while always a favorite honeymoon destination, it has become a popular wedding destination as well. The hotel's facilities are concentrated on the northeast section of the island and the hub of the resort is the marina on Sprat Bay. The rest of the island has pristine beaches and manicured trails that have been carved by the hotel through the mountainous terrain and secluded coves. You can reach Peter Island only by water or helicopter. The island is a terrific day-trip destination for visits to Tortola and a popular anchorage site as well.

A Brief History

In 1493, Christopher Columbus sailed through this region on his second voyage. He named these untouched islands after St. Ursula's 11,000 followers who chose death in fourth-century Cologne rather than submit to marauding Huns. Note that the channel in which these islands lie is not named for him but rather for the buccaneer Francis Drake and that several other islands are named for those privateers who routinely hid along the countless nooks and bays waiting for their chance to attack the treasure-laden Spanish ships.

By the late 17th century pirates gave way to planters from Germany who intended to establish a large settlement here, having failed to do so in nearby Danish-owned St. Thomas. The soil here did not allow for sugar cane plantations, but planters from Tortola did establish cotton plantations worked by slaves. The decline of the plantation system combined with the abolition of slavery led to the complete decline of Peter Island, which reverted to its natural primitive state.

THE WRECK OF THE RHONE

It was at Peter Island that the British RMS *Rhone* initially sought shelter from a fierce hurricane in 1897. The captain then decided to make a run for open waters but crashed on rocks off nearby Salt Island, where it has become the most popular scuba diving site in the area.

In the 1920s a few tobacco plantations were established but the island remained virtually uninhabited until the late 1960s, when Norwegian millionaire Peter Smedwig fell in love with it and purchased most of the land. He shipped in a group of luxury A-frame chalets and building materials from Norway and assembled them on Spray Bay, along with a clubhouse and marina.

It's incredible to think, when looking at the resort today, that in 1969 there was no water supply, no electricity and no roads on Peter Island. In fact, Sprat Bay had to be dredged to reclaim land from a coral reef on which tons of sand, rock and fill were piled. The original 32 rooms and some hotel facilities stand on this reclaimed area. Upon Smedwig's death in 1979, the resort was purchased by a Michigan-based corporation. They have upgraded many of the facilities and added new amenities, but have not lost sight of Smedwig's concept of a small, luxurious and tasteful resort.

Peter Island Resort
6470 East Johns Crossing #490
Mailbox 4149
Duluth, GA 30097
☎ (770) 476-3723
Deluxe
Closed September

 There are only 52 guest rooms and four private villas at the resort. Two were completed in 2004. Because Peter Island was badly damaged by Hurricane Hugo in 1989, virtually every resort facility that existed at that time was rebuilt and all have been refurbished again in the decade since. The 32 original rooms, called "Ocean View," are housed in two-story poolside A-frame cottages. Spacious, they have separate bedrooms, sitting areas and full master bathrooms. French doors lead to a private patio or terrace.

An additional 20 "Junior Suites" were added in 1984. Deluxe, they are housed in five bi-level bluestone and cedar buildings tucked behind palms and seagrape trees just above Deadman's Beach. From the windows, guests have spectacular views of the "pirate" islands in the near distance. Here you'll find Spanish-tiled baths with Jacuzzi tubs for two, oversized showers, comfortable sitting areas and private terraces or balconies. Lower-level rooms have a glass-roofed sun parlor that allows sun to light the two lounge chairs in the room.

Peter Island

All guest rooms are air-conditioned and also have ceiling fans. They feature high ceilings, light woods, wicker and rattan, as well as bright, colorful fabrics and wall hangings that make them warm and inviting. Manicured flowering plants and trees encircle all the buildings.

The resort's four exclusive villas are set on hillsides above Spray Bay. **The Hawk's Nest** has three bedrooms, four baths, a spacious living room with a media area and a kitchenette that is fully equipped. The large sun deck has a dipping pool. **The Crow's Nest** (four bedrooms) and the **Falcon's Nest** and **Raven's Nest** (each with six bedrooms) have large living rooms, king-size or twin beds, deep soaking bathtubs, separate showers, fully equipped kitchens and dining areas and private swimming pools. The spacious deck and patio areas offer panoramic views of the channel. Saving the best for last, each of these villas has a personal steward/chef and the use of an island rover. They are truly special.

There are two **restaurants** at the resort. The chef, a native Tortolian, has been here for over 30 years. **Tradewinds**, the main dining area has indoor and open-patio dining. Breakfast, served on the patio, is a sumptuous buffet with eggs, pancakes, bagels and smoked salmon, deli meats and fruits. An à la carte selection and continental breakfast are also available. The dinner menu at Tradewinds changes nightly. It showcases seasonal ingredients and contemporary dishes with Asian and Italian culinary influences. Recent menus started with carpaccio smoked salmon, char-grilled vegetable salad and banana cinnamon soup. A house specialty is the "Island Fisherman's Ciopino," which blends local fish and seafood in a garlicky tomato-vegetable broth. Potato-crusted wild seabass, seared fillet of tuna marinated in a blend of soy sauce, rice wine vinegar and sesame oil and filet mignon are also favorites. The Saturday night buffets are very popular. They feature cold and hot foods, including salads, cold lobster, meats, fruits, vegetables and desserts.

Lunch and lighter dinner fare are served at **Deadman's Beach Bar and Grill**, a roof-covered open-air terrace eatery on the beach. There's a lunch buffet as well as burgers, sandwiches and hot dogs. A wood-burning oven turns out very good pizzas with a variety of toppings. Sunday at lunch a steel band sets the mood, and there is a West Indian buffet on Monday night. Once again, a steel band plays and often traditional jumbo stilt walkers join in the fun.

THE WHITE BAY PICNIC

A special lunch treat, the White Bay Picnic lunch is a gourmet packed lunch box delivered to guests at a specified time. White Bay is the farthest beach from the hotel. The lunch can be delivered anywhere on the island.

A Caribbean tea is served each afternoon with a variety of iced teas and homemade banana bread and cookies.

Peter Island Resort has a renowned wine cellar. Every Thursday night a special wine dinner is served in the private room near Tradewinds.

Room rates include full American dining plans (all meals included).

Peter Island

Island Sites & Activities

Deadman's Beach is the heart of the resort and you'll spend many of your daylight hours here or in its waters. The recreation hut has a full complement of Hobie Cat sailboats, Sunfish and Laser sailboats, sea kayaks, windsurf boards, snorkel gear and water toys. Guests can sign out any of the above. You can snorkel at Deadman's, but the reef is better at **Little Deadman's Beach**, which adjoins Deadman's, or at **White Bay** on the southern shore. The island in the distance is **Dead Chest**. You can sail to it and snorkel there.

There are four other beaches on Peter Island. **Little Deadman's Bay** is a popular spot for sunning and yacht watching. The resort provides beach lounges for daytrippers here. **Honeymoon**, an intimate beach, has only two lounge chairs beneath a single thatch umbrella. It's a romantic hideaway. **Big Reef Bay Beach** stretches three-quarters of a mile. Its shallow reef is great for beach combing. A hiking trail winds along this palm-lined beach. White Bay is on the island's southern shore. The islands in the distance are Norman and St. Johns.

There are over two-dozen dive sites nearby.

The resort staff will arrange scuba diving trips, deep sea-fishing jaunts and daysails/snorkeling trips for an extra charge.

If you prefer, wile away the sunny daylight hours at poolside. The irregularly shaped good-sized swimming pool is on a terrace behind the main building. It has a sun deck and is adjacent to the cocktail lounge and dining room.

You can work up a sweat on one of the four Tru-flex tennis courts nestled in a grove of palm trees on Deadman's Beach. Two can be lighted for night play. The fitness center is another popular spot. It has stationery bicycles, treadmills, stair climbers and a fixed-weight machine. If you overdo it, arrange for a relaxing massage. The resort's spa, on Big Reef Beach, is a state-of-the-art facility of over 13,000 square feet. Built of stone and local woods with lots of sunlight and natural tones, it has its own pool and private patios. There are 10 indoor treatment suites, hydrotherapy tubs and a private steam room. Treatments include scrubs, massages, facials, body wraps and hair and nail services. Movement classes are offered and there is a meditation area.

By the way, the name Deadman's Bay comes from the fact that it faces Dead Chest Island, which figured in the tale of 15 pirates fighting over a bottle of rum.

TREASURE ISLAND

Visible from White Bay is Norman Island, the setting for Robert Louis Stevenson's tale, *Treasure Island*. It would seem that young Stevenson's uncle sailed these waters and regaled his nephew with tales of pirates, treasure-laden caves and rum bottles.

A half-dozen good hiking trails lead to ruins of an old settlement, to hilltops overlooking the channel and through garden-like areas. A fleet of mountain bikes are available if you prefer to pedal.

After Dark

Evening action centers around the cocktail lounge at poolside where a local calypso group or steel band plays for listening and dancing. Other guests head to the air-conditioned library/game

Peter Island

room to read, play chess or backgammon, or watch a movie on the oversized set.

Getting There

From Tortola

 The **Peter Islander Ferries**, 65-foot luxury motor-yachts, cross the Sir Francis Drake Channel from the island to Road Town 10 times each day. The trip takes 20 minutes. Guests of the resort don't pay for this service. Pick-up service at Beef Island/Tortola airport or the Road Town Ferry Dock is included in your room rate.

Peter Island is a terrific daytrip for those staying on Tortola. You can hop the Peter Islander Ferry for $15. The fee is waived if you have dinner on the island. Bring your own snorkel gear. Many daysail/snorkel ships anchor here.

From St. Thomas

Peter Island Resort offers pick-up and ferry service from St. Thomas to the island several days a week. There is an additional charge for this service.

Jost Van Dyke

Like a mischievous sibling, Jost Van Dyke has a different personality than Tortola and Virgin Gorda. It's the "party island," thanks to scores of restaurants and watering holes that stay open late and cater to merrymakers from the charter boats anchored offshore. The anchorages here are extremely popular. Jost Van Dyke's best-known resident, Foxy (Callwood) keeps the island lively. He organizes wooden boat regattas, his concerts feature such

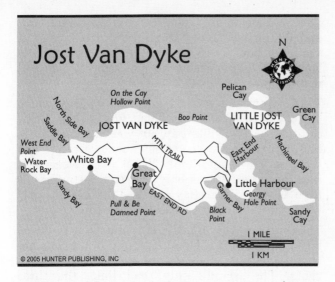

well-known performers as Burning Spear and his lavish parties on New Year's Eve and other holidays are lots of fun.

Named for a Dutch pirate, Jost (Yost) Van Dyke is west of Tortola, but is closest (four miles) to St. John, USVI. A long, narrow, hilly island, Jost Van Dyke has 211 residents, most of whom live in the village at Great Harbour. There is a church and a school, a few shops, colorful bars and eateries. The island is laid-back by day and cars, electricity and telephones are recent additions.

Most of the island is uninhabited. Whether you visit Jost Van Dyke for a day, or if you decide to stay for a few days, you'll spend most of your time at the three lively anchorages, with their pristine beaches and tiny settlements. Until recently, virtually all visitors to the island stayed aboard charter boats. There were hardly any places to stay on the island and there are still only a few. Some villas have been built to augment the two small hotels and campgrounds.

Jost Van Dyke

The settlements are Great Harbour, Little Harbour and White Bay. **Great Harbour** is the largest. A sheltered bay, it is where the ferries dock and is home to the greatest number of colorful bars and restaurants.

To the west of Great Harbour is **White Bay**, which has one of the BVI's most beautiful beaches. A taxi can take you to White Bay, but you can easily walk and that will allow you to see how lovely Jost Van Dyke is. The islands' only "hotel" (six cottages) is here and the island's only gourmet restaurant is here as well. White Bay also has the island's only watersports center and a water trampoline.

The third anchorage, **Little Harbour**, is a sheltered lagoon to the east of Great Harbour. It is a calm anchorage with a small marina and several restaurants. The island's only road links the three settlements.

There are several tiny cays off the east coast: **Little Jost Van Dyke** was once inhabited but is not at this time; **Diamond Cay** has a small marina and Foxy's newest restaurant; **Sandy Cay** and **Sandy Spit** are both uninhabited, but many yachts anchor near them for they have excellent snorkeling.

Getting There

 You can visit only by boat and the regular ferry service operates only during daylight hours. There is daily service from Tortola's West End. **New Horizon Ferry Service**, ☎ (284) 495-9278, has a half-dozen crossings daily. The first leaves West End at 9 am. The last ferry from Jost Van Dyke leaves at 4:30 pm. A group of six or more can charter a New Horizon ferry for a dinner trip. **Jost Van Dyke Ferry Service**, ☎ (284) 494-2997, begins at 7 am

and their last daily return leaves Jost Van Dyke at 4 pm. Check all schedules. They change.

Weekend service from St. Thomas and St. John is offered by **Interisland Boat Services**, ☎ (284) 495-4166.

Sunup to Sundown

 Great Harbour's beach is a beehive of activity but most of it is at the bars and restaurants and not on the sand. If you enjoy watersports, head to **White Bay Beach**, where you can rent gear, a lounge chair or one of the hammocks strung between the palm trees. There's a water trampoline here and you can rent water bikes, kayaks, jet boats, banana sleds, snorkel gear, windsurf boards and Sunfish from **BVI Land and Sea Adventures**, ☎ 492-2269, whose office is at the beach. They are open 9 am-5 pm daily. They also organize dinghy and kayak tours around Jost Van Dyke pointing out the natural beauty as well as the island's history and folklore.

Old trails connect all parts of the island. Since there are very few cars, islanders still use them. You can visit the foamy bubbling pool at the island's east end, where the seawater forms a natural Jacuzzi. You can walk to Little Jost, but you'll need a boat to get to Sandy Cay, where the beach and snorkeling are excellent. In the fall and winter you can watch whales and dolphins in the crystal-clear waters nearby.

Jost Van Dyke

Best Places to Stay

There are very few places to stay on Jost Van Dyke and most are quite rustic. If amenities such as air conditioning, cable TVs, hair dryers, Internet connections, even telephones, are important to you, be sure to ask when booking. Ask about credit cards as well. At this writing, only the Sandcastle Hotel accepts them, but change is coming to Jost Van Dyke.

Hotels are generally cheaper here then on Tortola and Virgin Gorda. "Moderate" means $100-$200 nightly.

Sandcastle Hotel
White Bay
☎ (284) 495-9888
www.sandcastle-bvi.com
Moderate
Six beachfront cottages, beach bar and gourmet restaurant.

Sea Crest Inn
Great Harbour
☎ (284) 495-9024
Inexpensive
Four beachfront, one-bedroom apartments with air conditioning and kitchenettes.

Sandy Ground Estates
Baker's Bay
☎ (284) 494-3391
www.sandyground.com
Moderate
Eight villas, two and three bedrooms, full kitchens, terrace. Rents by the week primarily.

White Bay Villas
White Bay
☎ (410) 571-6192
www.jostvandyke.com
Moderate
Three private villas, one, two, three bedrooms, fully equipped kitchens, nicely furnished. Weekly rentals.

White Bay Campground
White Bay
☎ (284) 495-9312

On a beautiful beach, cabins, tents and bare sites near the villas above as well as restaurants. There are showers/toilets.

Best Places to Eat

 Restaurants here are quite small. They serve West Indian food with emphasis on freshly caught shellfish and fish. They cook "to the house," so you must reserve for dinner by 4 pm. They do not accept credit cards for the most part, so inquire when making your reservation. They are all informal, except for Sandcastle, where you need collared shirts and trousers for men and casual chic attire for women.

Great Harbour

Foxy's, ☎ (284) 495-9258. Foxy is a BVI institution and he often plays guitar and sings calypso. The restaurant is open for lunch and dinner daily. Barbecue on Friday and Saturday nights. Live bands too. Accepts credit cards.

Ali Baba's, ☎ (284) 495-9280, is near the customs house. Open for all three meals. The rum punch here packs a wallop.

Club Paradise, ☎ (284) 495-9267, is a colorful beachside spot serving burgers and sandwiches for lunch and fresh fish for dinner.

Wendell's World, ☎ (284) 495-9259, is open from 8 am to 11 pm, but it's best at lunch, when they serve delicious honey-dipped chicken.

White Bay

Sandcastle, ☎ (284) 495-9888, is the island's only gourmet eatery. There is a set menu each night. Dinner is served at 7 pm and you must reserve by 4 pm. Candlelit tables, international foods, good service. Soggy Dollar Bar nearby serves lunch and breakfast. Try the "Pain Killer." You'll sleep well.

Jewel's Snack Shop, ☎ (284) 495-9286, offers burgers, hot dogs, fries, ice cream and soft drinks. Open 11 am to 4 pm.

Little Harbour

Abe's Little Harbour, ☎ (284) 495-9329, is a native bar and restaurant serving fish, conch, spare ribs and chicken. Pig roast Wednesday nights in season.

Harris' Place, ☎ (284) 495-9302, serves all three meals. Local seafood and West Indian specialties.

Foxy's Taboo, ☎ (284) 495-9258, is actually on Diamond Cay at the island's east end. Open for all three meals, it specializes in Mediterranean fare.

Shopping

Two shops you'll enjoy browsing in are **Foxy's** (Great Harbour) and **Sandcastle's Soggy Dollar** (White Bay). They offer tropical clothing, T-shirts and gifts.

After Dark

The bars and restaurants listed above stay open late and much of the nightlife centers around them. **Foxy's Tamarind** in Great Harbour stays open late and has music every night. Special events are also held there.

Anegada

Anegada stands out for a variety of reasons. It is not on the Sir Francis Drake Channel, as are most of the other islands. The northernmost of the BVIs, Anegada is 20 miles northeast of Tortola. In addition, it is a coral island, while all of the others are volcanic. In many ways Anegada is more like a Pacific atoll than a Caribbean island. Its flora and fauna are unique and wild orchids are commonplace.

Only 15 square miles, its highest point is only 28 feet above the sea. You can see how it got its name – Anegada means "Drowned Land." The island has lovely beaches on its northern and western shores, but its most unusual feature is the spectacular 13-mile coral reef that encircles the island.

Warning: Don't even think about sailing here – 300 ships have been caught on this treacherous reef. They are now dive sites.

The 250 residents of Anegada live in two small communities, **The Settlement** and **Loblolly Bay**. Most residents are fishermen.

Getting There

 There is no scheduled ferry service at this writing but many daysail operators on Virgin Gorda offer trips to Anegada. There are also daytrips from Tortola. The best way to get to Anegada is to fly there from Tortola's Beef Island Airport. The flight takes 12 minutes. **Clair Aero** has a flight on Monday, Wednesday, Friday and Sunday, ☎ (284) 495-2271. Two helicopter services offer Anegada day trips. **Island Helicopters**, ☎ (284) 499-2663, and **Fly Anegada**, ☎ (284) 495-1797, offer charter service.

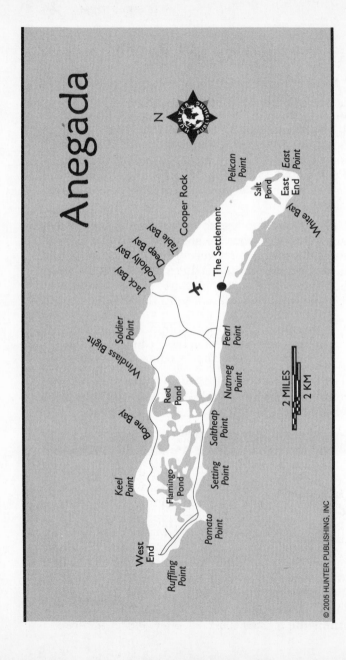

Anegada

N

West End
Ruffling Point
Keel Point
Bone Bay
Flamingo Pond
Red Pond
Windlass Bight
Soldier Point
Jack Bay
Loblolly Bay
Deep Bay
Table Bay
Cooper Rock
Pomato Point
Setting Point
Saltheap Point
Nutmeg Point
Pearl Point
The Settlement
Pelican Point
Salt Pond
East End
East Point
White Bay

2 MILES
2 KM

Best Places to Stay

There are a handful of hotels on the island.

Anegada Reef Hotel & Cottages
Setting Point
☎ (284) 495-8002
www.anegadareef.com

 This is the largest hotel on the island. It has 20 motel-style rooms that are air-conditioned. There are also two-bedroom cottages at this informal beachfront complex. The owner arranges fishing, scuba and bonefishing jaunts. There is a beach bar and a restaurant that specializes in grilled seafood, including the Anegada lobster. Food is included in the rate.

Neptune's Treasure Guest Rooms
Bender's Bay
☎ (284) 495-9439
neptunestreasures@surfbvi.com
Moderate
Best known for its restaurant, Neptune's has added a few single and double rooms. They are air-conditioned but do not have kitchenettes. There is an additional charge for maid service.

Anegada Beach Cottages
Pomato Point
☎ (284) 495-9234
www.anegadabeachcottages.com
Inexpensive
These cottages are more upscale than those at Neptune. They have separate sitting areas and comfortable island-style furnishings.

Anegada has three **campgrounds**. You can reserve a tent or a bare site. For specifics:

Anegada Beach	☎ (284) 495-9466
Mac's Campgrounds	☎ (284) 495-8020
Neptune's Treasure	☎ (284) 495-9439

Best Places to Eat

Anegada Reef Hotel
Setting Point
☎ (284) 495-8002 VHF #16

 The restaurant, on a stunning beach, serves all three meals. Lunch (12:30-2) features burgers, salads and sandwiches. Dinner (from 7:30 pm) offers a choice of freshly caught barbecued lobsters, ribs, fish and chicken. Dinner reservations must be made before 4 pm.

Big Bamboo
Loblolly Bay
☎ (284) 495-2019 VHF #16
Moderate, no credit cards

On Anegada's north shore, The Big Bamboo specializes in West Indian food. The lobster, conch and fish are freshly caught and delicious. Lunch only.

Neptune's Treasure
Bender's Bay
☎ 459-9439 VHF #16
Inexpensive, no credit cards

Bender's Bay is between Pomato and Saltheap Point (west of The Settlement). The owners are fishermen who catch, cook and serve locally caught seafood. Same menu for lunch and dinner.

Lobster Trap
The Settlement (waterfront)
☎ (284) 495-9466 VHF #16
Inexpensive, no credit cards

In a lovely garden, The Lobster Trap specializes in lobster. The island favorite is served in a variety of ways but the barbecued lobsters stand out. Serves lunch and dinner. Reserve for dinner by 4 pm.

Sunup to Sundown

Snorkeling and diving are as good as anywhere in the BVI. Fishlife is abundant and shipwrecks are easily seen, with 138 charted. *The Paramatta,* at 35 feet, is broken into two parts and overgrown with elkhorn coral. *The Rocus,* a Greek freighter carrying the strange cargo of animal bones that now litter the deck, lies at 40 feet. A noosje on the ship shows where the disgraced captain hanged himself.

Over the years many old coins and other artifacts have been swept ashore. An island resident collected these treasures and started a museum. **The Pomato Point Museum** also has Arawak Indian artifacts. **Cow Wreck Bay** was named for the cow bones that were washed ashore for years after a wreck. The bones were used to make buttons.

The island has many pristine coral beaches. Beachcombing, snorkeling, bonefishing and deep-sea fishing are readily available.

Although you can rent a car from **J + L Jeep Rentals** at ☎ (284) 495-3138, the most popular way to get around the island is to rent a bike; ☎ (284) 495-8027. There is also taxi service. (tel #?)

Walking is not strenuous since Anegada is so flat. The **BVI National Parks Trust** has declared much of the island off-limits to settlement. These acres are reserved for birds and other wildlife. The Trust has established a flamingo colony in the salt ponds and a bird sanctuary that protects several varieties of herons, ospreys and terns. The interior part of the island is a preserved habitat for Anegada's animal population of some 2,000 wild goats, donkeys and cattle.

If you're lucky, you'll see the rare rock iguanas, fierce-looking but harmless reptiles that can grow up to five feet in length and weigh up to 20 pounds. These very shy creatures have lived on Anegada for thousands of years.

Shopping

Shopping is limited but there are a handful of stops. **Pat's Pottery and Art** features locally made pottery and crafts. **V&J's Souvenir and Gift Shop** also sells local pottery along with inexpensive jewelry and clothing. **Pam's Kitchen** sells jams, sauces and colorful items for the kitchen. **Dotsie's Bakery** sells freshly baked breads and pastries. The **Anegada Reef Hotel** has a gift shop and boutique for T-shirts and the like.

Guana Island

A privately owned island, Guana is much larger than Necker. Its 840 acres lie off Tortola's northeast coast. Once a Quaker sugar plantation, it is now home to the exclusive Guana Island Club. There are no public amenities on Guana and access to the island is limited to hotel guests, who are picked up by launch at the Beef Island dock.

Guana Island is not an anchorage.

Guana Island Club
Box 32, Road Town
Tortola, BVI
☎ (284) 494-2354/(914) 967-6050
www.guana.com
Deluxe (all inclusive)

 The club only accommodates 30 guests, who are housed in seven cottages set on a ridge and scattered through the cleared grounds. There is a special beachfront cottage that has its own pool and guests have the use of a golf cart to reach the main house.

The grounds here are exceptional, for the island is both a nature reserve and wildlife sanctuary. Over 50 species of birds have been identified and several endangered birds are cared for here.

Rooms are large and comfortable but not lavish. They reflect their Quaker roots with homemade bed-spreads, cane and wicker furniture and lots of native stone. Each has a private terrace offering sensational views of the Sir Francis Drake Channel.

Rates include three meals daily, afternoon tea and cocktails and wines at lunch and dinner. There is no marina or public restaurant so the mix of guests is very important. Meals can be eaten at large communal tables or at smaller intimate ones. Dinners are served by candlelight. The food is prepared in West Indian fashion and menus often depend on the catch of the day.

There are seven beaches on Guana Island, two of which are accessible only by water. You can snorkel, windsurf or sail to them. There is one tennis court, a croquet field and lots of interesting hikes through the nature reserve.

The Guana Island Club takes reservations for individual guests, but it is also possible to rent the entire island and many corporations do so. The resort is closed in September and October to allow for scientific research.

Guana Island Club has reluctantly started to accept credit cards. Master Card and Visa only. The dress code at dinner is casual chic.

Guana Island

Saba Rock Island

Tiny Saba Rock Island is one of a handful of scarcely inhabited islands in Virgin Gorda's North Sound. Other islands nearby include Eustatia and Necker (both private), Prickly Pear, which has a restaurant and is a national park site, and Mosquito Island, which is a popular anchorage. Its resort, Drake's Anchorage, is closed at this writing.

Saba Rock Island Resort
North Sound
☎ (284) 495-9966
www.sabarock.com
Closed September
Expensive

 Saba Rock's accommodations include one- and two-bedroom villas, as well as suites and studio units. All rooms have water views, are air-conditioned and have satellite TVs. Continental breakfast is included in your rate. Surrounded by the blue waters of the Sound, guests can sail, windsurf, snorkel and paddle to their heart's content. There is a small sandy beach. The resort is accessible only by boat so guests hop the North Sound Express on Beef Island. At the Bitter End ferry dock (Virgin Gorda), the Saba Rock Island ferry picks them up for the short ride to the resort.

You can sail or motor to larger Prickly Pear Island nearby. The Sand Box, a casual beach bar is a popular spot.

The restaurant, on the water's edge, serves pub fare at lunch and all-you-can-eat buffets and grilled fish, steak and lobsters at dinner. There are steel bands, dancing and special event nights. Anchored yachtsmen join in the fun.

Necker Island

Necker Island
Box 1091, The Valley
Virgin Gorda (☎ (284) 494-2757; ☎ (800) 557-4255
www.neckerisland.com
Deluxe (all inclusive)

 Several small outer islands are privately owned. Necker Island, a 74-acre hideaway in North Sound, is one. Owned by Sir Richard Branson, it houses a luxurious resort that can accommodate only 26 guests. Individual reservations are not an option, for Necker is available only to groups. Corporate meetings and intimate weddings are the norm here.

Buildings peek out from the colorful tropical plants and trees as your ferry approaches the island. All the buildings resemble Balinese temples. There are 10 rooms in the Great House, including a master suite with a rooftop terrace and Jacuzzi. Three other pavilions nearby have one-bedroom suites with open-air sitting areas and dining rooms.

The Great House terrace and dining areas are where guests gather for cocktails and to enjoy the meals prepared by a gourmet chef. Menus are heavy with local fish, fresh fruits and vegetables (special requests honored) and all meals are served informally. There are often beach barbecues and theme nights. There is a sushi bar too.

Necker has two tennis courts, two pools, and three beaches, one of which has an aqua-trampoline. Guests can snorkel over nearby reefs or sail to others nearby. There are windsurf boards, sailboats, kayaks and water skis. The newest addition is the spa, built into a cliffside.

The Great House lounge has comfortable sofas and oversized chairs where guests can read, watch a DVD on a large-screen TV (none in guest rooms) or play board games or pool. The staff is large, friendly and helpful. The dress code at dinner is casual chic.

Index

Index

Index